Calcutta Song

Calcutta Song

Life, love and learning in a city of dreams

Joe Winter

Peridot Press

Published 2013

by Peridot Press Ltd,
12 Deben Mill Business Centre, Old Maltings Approach,
Melton, Woodbridge IP12 1BL
Tel: +44 (0) 1394 389850
Email: enquiries@peridot.co.uk
Website: www.peridot.co.uk

© Joe Winter 2012

ISBN: 978 1 908095 70 1
eISBN: 978 1 908095 80 0

Printed and bound in Great Britain
by Ashford Colour Press

First published in 2012 by Sahitya Samsad, Kolkata.
Poems and poem-translations by kind permission of
Anvil Press, London. Sonnets: 'Guest and Host' 2003;
'Grass' by Jibanananda Das: 'Naked Lonely Hand' 2003; excerpts
from 'Gitanjali' 106 by Rabindranath Tagore: 'Song Offerings' 2000.

FOREWORD

This is not a travel book but one of exploration. Calcutta, that became Kolkata in 2001, a little over halfway through my stay there, almost by chance became the gateway to a journey of discovery. If one can learn of the world through a place, and in so doing, come to terms a little more with one's place in the world, the pages that follow offer an example. But in a sense that is neither here nor there: what is immediate is the foremost city of the state of West Bengal.* It used to be the foremost city of India, and has a universal quality still.

Founded towards the end of the seventeenth century, from 1772 to 1912 it was India's capital. Trade, intellectual life, festival shone. When the capital was moved to Delhi its inner pulse stayed as strong, and throughout the twentieth century it was characterised in part by a sense of ferment, a place where ideas might catch and seethe, even at times boil over. In the arts, as a centre for university work, as a stamping-ground for political energies, beneath a slow-moving exterior the city is alight with risk, the danger of the new. And beneath all, the trace of a numinous quality is never absent, that blazes up each autumn in the ten-day festival of Durga Puja.

Perhaps the last place on Earth where the worship of a mother goddess is so much felt, so free, from the smallest

*As I write the state is moving to change to its Bengali name, Paschimbanga.

7

village to its nerve-centre of some sixteen million, the state brims with the beauty of submission. How much did I learn then, how much my dry English soul drank in! That festival is the template of these pages, a pattern that may govern the assembly of the whole. Other goddesses are celebrated too, and there is the great secular event of the Book Fair, together with any number of historical personages, that stand behind the daily panorama of the city.

But the state is not an island. This is a book about India. About how an Englishman came to know it in his way, and about the country itself, a glimpsed impression. If something of its unique quality may fleetingly catch the reader's eye, as it seemed to do the writer's, over a stay of a dozen years, a private story may be allowed to tap on the door of the public domain.

JW 2011

1

In March 1994 I went to India for a few years. I thought it was going to be three or so, but three turned into twelve. I thought I would travel and live here and there, a few weeks or months at a time; but starting in Calcutta, after two weeks the decision seemed to be made to stay there, if the city would have me. She did; and gave me a hard time, and a true time. What was I in touch with? Back now in England for two years, I discover – from a chance remark of someone's – that I may as well speak now, and that the city will let me. A commentary will follow, trivia for the most part, of sights and sounds and sensations, light and dark and people, a dot in time. Anyone who has travelled knows one can run at things, take in too much. A short chapter at a time I hope will entertain, and open up the dot, and admit whoever is interested to a sequence of richness and strangeness and lightness, a journey made in the dark across a threshold.

A few years before my return Calcutta became Kolkata; but it was not Kolkata to which I went, not knowing a soul, in '94. I shall use the older name here, with apologies to those who may feel it inappropriate. I enjoy the use of the new name for matters of the present; but this is of the past, and while there is overlap, for the sake of convenience and my own writing's authenticity, I'll stay with the old one. Kolkata, the Bengali title that has taken its place on the map, may not be averse to letting its departed sister live on a little in print in the recall of one who is, after all, an older person.

I was fifty-one when I went. I remember the appalled realisation, as I left London, that I had no keys. I'd given them all up, the house to my wife – we had already been separated for a couple of years – and the flat I rented in Southall to the agent. I had no keys. Time is different, there's room for more to happen in it. Or, as it seemed then, less: I was travelling on the skimpiest of assumptions, that not to know what one was doing was a valid way of doing it. The decision had been many years in the making, the separation far and away the hardest part of it. It had been an amicable one, and I felt my wife (as she still was in name) was with me in my intent, our two grown sons also. But I had to make a clean break. It had come to me about twenty years before that I'd spread my wings when the boys were older. Miraculously at fifty I was awarded an early retirement pension from school-teaching – a loophole the authorities later closed – and it was possible. But why the break?

I was resolved to live for a good time in different parts of the so-called developing world. I wrote poetry; it had something to do with it. I thought I'd start in India, over three or four years write a book of poems, come back for a year to the UK, think, consolidate, 'supply'-teach, try to publish, and go and do the same, in no particular order, in a Muslim country, in China, in a Central American country, and a sub-Saharan country or countries of Africa. I'd spent a summer holiday going round Zimbabwe five years before, and India the following summer, which told me where to start: the mix of old and new up and down India had got hold of me. I heard it as a sound and knew I could continue to do so. I'd like to think that it wasn't being a poet that took me there to stay, but being alive and in a world where it was possible to go a little along the way to see how the other half lived and what it was. The presumption in all this is fairly mind-boggling, not least in the insouciant way one decides one will go and live here or live there, as if a place the other side of the world were there for one's convenience. So I had a rough scheme of about twenty years; and started in Calcutta only because in my earlier summer trip I'd visited the other main metropolises, Delhi, Bombay and Madras (the latter two now Mumbai and Chennai), but had not made it to the City of Dreadful Night.

Kipling had called it that; but I went, I swear, with an open mind. I knew something of the Hindu tradition of retirement to the forest at fifty or so, after a long stretch as householder, to meditate and to be. I wasn't doing that but a mid-life upping of sticks resonated. Certain friends said I went to find squalor but there was no more than a germ of truth in that, and it wasn't for squalor's sake. What drew me more was Time. We're lucky in England to be surrounded by a thousand years or so of the tangible stream of change, but that's in comparison with the US and such. What I'd felt in my preliminary trip to India was an older Time, not so much in the temples as in the air. This was very much part of 'the other half' of the world, and naturally of myself as well. It all went together, Hindu tradition and a city notorious for its poverty and a country where nothing is ever forgotten. And, I suppose, a need to discover whether I was still alive, or too deeply in the groove of the pattern I knew to do anything about it. I won't deny a macho element to the enterprise nor a more telling vein of immaturity, a selfish disregard for my wife of twenty-four years. She agreed to it all but it wasn't what she had in mind at marriage. But for me, nevertheless, it was a going forward.

When we split up I went to live in Southall, a mainly Punjabi area of West London. It was near my work in Ealing, it was cheap, it breathed the subcontinent. I was absorbed very little into its current yet to be close by may have prepared me a touch for what lay ahead. In the park in the afternoon men would congregate to talk. It was an alliance with the open air I was to see a deal more of later: the simplest of ways of being, but not one that went on in Wimbledon Common, where you'd get shouted at by golfers if you stood around. I'd lived in Wimbledon (down the hill from the Common) for two decades or more and it felt like forever. I'd taught English in London comprehensive schools and relished it, the dynamic of the young who are changing too fast for any veneer to settle, and their madcap humour. I also liked teaching words: how to write them, how to think with them, how to hear the tune beneath them, how not to be dictated to by them. This last is an offshoot of the first three and conveyed, if that is the word, undeliberately, unless one is studying an advertisement. But it's there in the background of what one is doing, the drop of sanity in the flood-tide of essays and stories, coursework and talks; and it was this, too, I think I felt in what little I knew of the ancient reason of India.

Its opposite is all too well known, the caste system, the endless mantras, the over-literal emphasis on, as it may be, repeating a god's name. And I had some slight idea – that was to be filled out all too tellingly and yet still leave me ignorant in essence – of the dead hand of tradition. The warping of lives, the crushing of the girl-child, the owing of labour, the multiplication of debt. And the long pockets of corruption, that again I was to see in a never-ending stitch-up that still, because I was not Indian, I was never to feel next to the bone. I did not know if the sense I had of some countervailing reason, based more broadly and accurately, in overall human terms, than the West's columns of logic and frieze of public-spiritedness, was mere wish-fulfilment on my part. But I was on my way, not to research such things, but to be where they might or might not be in operation. I sensed a sanity in where I was going, as well as a closed mind, in larger measure than in the West. A dust-storm of swirling opposites, such as these and related to these, hovered in my mind before I touched down at Dum Dum Airport. But it was all in the background. In front was a place and people no different from myself. But I knew nothing, and no-one, again a child.

2

I started off in a Baptist guest-house that a couple of Danes I'd met on the flight were fixed up to stay at. It had a lovely garden that I rose early my first morning to sit in. Two or three crows were scavenging odds and bobs from the lawn, and I watched amazed as one tussled with a metal coat-hanger. It tried again and again to carry it off but the weight always took it back down to ground. And then it had the centre of gravity in its beak and tremulously gained height and flew over the wall. What kind of nest it was after God alone knew; but of one thing I had no doubt. Indian crows are cleverer.

I left after two weeks, as I had not come to India to share a dormitory and dinner-table with Christian priests, and set up in a narrow cheap room in a Sudder Street hotel. Sudder Street is the tourist centre of Calcutta and the Hotel Maria gave me a space to operate from, and read and write in, for eight months or so. It was an unprepossessing place, and a banal enough operation I gave my days to: wandering here and there, tracing the Bengali alphabet on my palm over coffee, getting on and off buses, finding my way. But I got to know quite a few people; and looking back a tremendous amount happened. One reason was I was in no rush; another perhaps that with a quarter-century behind me of career and children and paying bills, a path emerged, simply because I was not testing the limits as the young do but merely letting the city take me along. Though that was tiring enough at times.

I looked in on a chess tournament at one point and met a few shop-owners who took an interest in me. I used to take a bus out to a village where two of them lived and play chess all day in the weekends. There was a corpse one morning by the side of the road in the village: we passed it on the way to the community social room where we played, and again when we broke for lunch, and again when we left at six or so in the evening and it was near dark. The word was that it was a beggar and no-one wanted to incur the cremation cost. Before I boarded the bus back the authorities seemed to be taking the matter in hand. Much of the talk between games had centred on the dead man, who was known to the locals. I couldn't follow Bengali but what was said to me in English clarified a tone I'd picked up. These cheerful and generous people had the door shut in their minds about the body: a bad lot, a low incarnation with vice hanging around from a previous existence. But the shut door, if it was, didn't bother me. The image of the body on the other hand often has, lying all day in full view. I recounted the story to a group of Indians some time later: the general view was the same except for an economics professor who was furious with the company. "He might have been a better man than any of us!" he raged. But the others were not professors but tradespeople of one sort or another and disagreed.

I came to know Sudder Street in those eight months. There was a cobbler father and son on the pavement: the older man was forever commenting on his son's lack of skill. The younger took it in good part; but his father was indeed amazing. He used certain toes as extra fingers and stays in my mind as the professional nonpareil. He once showed me round his living space, a few square yards with the use of a basic bathroom and floor sleeping-space of a building by his pitch. I saw no wife. A year or so later visiting the street I saw the son who told me his father had died. He'd caught a cold. He was only ten years or so older than myself and had seemed a hardy character. There was a fat man who ran a stall he cleared with an agile vault every morning to get into position to sell. A seller of cheap wooden flutes haunted the tourists with enchanting snatches. Every evening someone would walk up behind me offering girls, boys, drugs. Once I heard him coming and before he started his basic-English spiel I said it for him in something like his voice: at once he said in a much better imitation of mine, "You selling?" He left me alone after that, a good moment to end on. In a café – the famous Blue Sky – an elderly newspaper-seller cried his wares at breakfast-time. I loved the quavering impeccable long 'a' in his 'Statesman!' It was a newspaper I was to write for later. In the garden of the Fairlawn Hotel in the street, where I spent a good few hundred hours all told, I met a nephew of Merchant, as in Merchant and Ivory, who asked me to write a script for a Sudder Street film. But when I told him the sort of thing I anticipated, with moments from the lives of people such as the above, he said no, no, it had to be about the marvellous young people from Germany and America and God knows where who thronged the place and worked as volunteers at various Mother Teresa institutions and whom I tended simply to blank out. Generally I couldn't stand them. Inappropriately revealing clothes, T-shirts with slogans such as 'I've got PMT – ignore me', and sentimental pity for the street kids – who brilliantly played them, changing personality to suit the mark – well, I told Mr Merchant no. He seemed to see the Indians as incidentals. No doubt his commercial instinct was sound.

Sudder Street. I often revisited it later, and have never really left the Fairlawn garden. I used to translate poems there with the aid of bottles of gaseous beer, or sit through monsoon bursts under one of its slight shelters. People recognised me in the street up to the time I left India. A sensitive spiv in his mid-twenties who worked at the Blue Sky when I left I'd known as a twelve-year-old boy taking orders there from all and sundry with aplomb. The memories flood up of a dumb, gesticulating humorist, of a man who slept on the pavement with dogs, of a friendly, slightly bewildered young man from Bihar who did menial jobs in the Hotel Maria, Bulle by name and Bullet to the world, of a middle-aged woman of the street to whom I never spoke yet who knew of my presence, and I hers, as if we were sister and brother ... switch off, switch off. Merely I was there.

Very early on I attended an informal meeting of amateur artists and writers in a country setting outside Calcutta to celebrate the first day of *Baisakh* (roughly 'Boy-shakh'), the first month in the Bengali cultural calendar. Here I was not a tourist or town-dweller and almost before I had begun my Sudder Street sojourn, felt a welcome from the land. I remembered the occasion in the first of a series of fifty sonnets I wrote over the next six years or so. I shall end each chapter with one of these, in sequence as they appeared. They tell a side of the story I can't put in prose. West Bengal is full of the goddess Durga, of whom more later, and my 'Lady of India' is to do with her, but not her. Who she is I know past knowing and not at all.

*L*ady of India, harbour to my soul,
  what would you ask of me? As voyaging
a mariner is held in water and light
to offer a prayer of thanks that he is home
though on his way; or a land-traveller
suddenly knows the ground-love of his Earth
and bending, touches grass and sand, to say
instinctive praises; so great Queen of Time,
I turn to you in words, who scarcely know you,
tremble before you, goddess terrible-strong
and smiling-kindly: here am I born again.
You recognise me and have sent companions,
poets and artists, friends of word and light,
to welcome in Baisakh in Krishnanagar.

3

Still at the beginning, I visited four Mother Teresa institutions with a view to learning something and adding structure to the day. I had taught in London up to a few days before the flight and thought remnants of a daily working pattern might be needed. I worked a couple of hours at a hostel for orphaned children, a little surprised to be the only man there, till a nun of the Mother's order had a word with me. "I'm sorry but you have to go." "What have I done?" "Nothing, but men can't work here." "Why not?" "I can't tell you." Later on I found out that at that particular refuge a young nun had fallen for and run off with a young chap from abroad, and the Mother had put the rule in place. It didn't operate a few doors away in the same building, where I spent the rest of the morning helping to look after severely retarded children. One boy of three or four wanted me to hold him up to a window so he could look out. He cried every time I put him down to relieve my arms. I asked if I could take him outside for a bit. Horror. "They don't go out." "What?" "The children are not allowed outside." It turned out there were two exceptions to the rule: the hospital, or an acclimatising walk preceding adoption. There were any number of toys and crayons and so on tucked away in cupboards and drawers. Gifts from abroad, unused. Children were being force-fed on their backs on the floor. I could have stayed but didn't. I went to a leper hostel under the same auspices outside Calcutta. Everyone sat on their beds, silent – apart from a severely ill man who lay on the floor making strange noises and insisted on clasping my hand. When I left I contributed a hundred rupees, then two or three pounds, and asked if it might be used for second-hand newspapers and magazines. "They can't read." "Maybe some can. And they can look at the pictures." "They don't want them." The fourth Teresa beacon of hope was little different.

There were any number of admirable young people from comparatively well-off countries doing good work in these and like sites. But for me it was off-track. I could give little and receive nothing. In a month or two however I found myself teaching a day a week at a state school in a town three hours away by packed train. These were full Wednesdays. It is almost with bared teeth that I recall the train; but the school was a place, however different from the plush classroom blocks I was used to in London, where I could be at ease. Whether thirty students to a classroom or a hundred and six, I was the same person in it, I suppose, as I had been before.

That is to say since I started teaching, back in '67. As I write in '08 I'm still going, back in England and full-time, and when I do finally hang up the duster, I'll know something of the land of the classroom, the great subcontinent of the teenage child. In a school I was not abroad. So I went to Kalinagar High School, on the outskirts of Krishnanagar, with a boys' class in three figures and another of seventy graceful sari-clad girls, many from poor farms; and despite the rigours of the journey I guess I woke up a touch. Looking back, it was like a step over a threshold, though most of me remained outside, engaging a deal more slowly with my new home.

I find myself reluctant to recount school anecdotes. It is a problem with "travel writing", cherry-picking, lighting upon something exotic and seizing on it, as if the strange quantity were not oneself. Whatever modicum of self-respect is left me after yielding to the suggestion of a friend that I write of my "experiences in India" – since I had thought the intuitive comment of poetry was for me the only way – I shall hang onto by not making capital out of the classroom. But I must say something to recognise the special quality of the places that took me on; and in Kalinagar High it was the quiet common sense of the staffroom that showed friendship but not excessive interest, people having work to do.

I have no such problems with the trains. Commuters, many on a journey such as mine six days a week instead of one, were amazing. There was a bridge school I longed to join. One of the four would sit, others if they were lucky, the back of a briefcase was the card-table, and they played in the most splendid isolation in the evenings going home. Once or twice, wildly jammed on a hot afternoon, I passed a mildly wicked hour or so imagining in turn everyone I knew in England pinned in the same mêlée. It filled the time. In the late evenings a down train – back to Calcutta – was often nearly empty. I remember a mad boy, a train urchin as it seemed, with a roll of plastic that may have been to sleep on, darting about the long deserted carriage making strange noises. Another time I was very nearly attacked by three youths. The central doors of the carriage were wide open to the night and there would have been no witnesses. More often people would want to talk with me, out of friendliness or curiosity or occasionally in a burning need to practise their English. I was hurtfully rude sometimes when the hint wasn't taken. But like India itself, the train story, once boarded, goes on and on: a sequence of beggars' songs and vendors' calls and intense snippets of conversation, a tolerance of children that is unimaginable in the West, an expressive aspect of the pain and ease of a land, a miasma, a blessing. I began to understand where the many gods come from, on my train journeys.

Here and there, in and around Calcutta, I visited households. I learnt to eat with my fingers (of the right hand), usually on a chair, at times cross-legged on the floor. In the latter position I tended to spill food, saddled with the least flexible of backs. No-one minded. In all my twelve years there I never mastered the art of drinking water from a bottle without admitting rim to lips. The pure tilt was beyond me. But I didn't mind (too much) trying and being laughed at, wet chin and chest blabbering my helplessness. Part of charging off somewhere in middle age is no doubt to find the child again. My actual childhood had been a reserved affair. If there was a trace in any sense at all of a second introduction to infancy, so to speak, the difference this time lay in the welcome around me.

A moment from my earlier 'listening' trip before I made

the move. I am in Hardwar, a holy town outside Delhi on the Ganga River (Ganges). There are about a hundred thousand people on the banks, in the river, receiving the prayers of priests, one with the great swirling god. Probably I'm the only white person there: at any rate, when I jump in (seizing a knotted rope as I go to find the way back by) there's a massive roar. I was to experience a certain cold-shouldering later on from urban intellectuals and others, but that shout of welcome never left me.

*L*ady, so many of your children
have chattered at me, blessed me with their eyes
while I, dumb-tongued, food-awkward
dither at the edge, perch beyond
in a white-and-pink elsewhere. Lady
I can tell you. Long ago
there shuddered down a path in space
a child in a stone. On the world
the sun ripened green, green branches
in an illusion of manhood. India take
the child from the stone. Burn
the guarantee of coldness from the skull ...
enough to tell and ask you this.
You shake your head, a fond indulgent mother.

4

I was of course reading. India is a vast hearthside of stories, gods, goddesses, disguise, love, war, cunning, family vicissitudes, promises and punishments, all the knockabout glory of power. From birth it warms the blood; and even to linger on a visit is to be singed by the flame. Rajagopalachari's miniature versions in English of the Ramayana and the Mahabharata were a starting-point that went off at a hazard in this direction and that, old stories mixing with new, so many and so often quickened by the presence of mythic ancestors who might have passed away last week. Their names come up in everyday conversation and newspaper headlines; they are part of how the land thinks; but more, they are dear, a treasured part of the extended family. Perhaps my most fortunate experience, early on, was to see a few far-flung stories off the page in rich cascade on a stage in a field.

It was the State Folk Theatre Festival, traditionally held in a village, and in '94 over four evenings at Karnajora near Raigunj in the rural heartland of West Bengal. Troupes had come from all parts of the state, including one from the north with an accent one and all said they couldn't understand. Conscious of the wild inappropriateness (but unable to resist) I thought of it as the Newcastle group. I was attached to a group of Calcutta MA students and their lecturer/leader, who each morning went over in detail what I'd seen the night before. In the field I didn't understand a word but was met at some level by a touch of epic.

It was tough. The entire village was there, several thousands sitting on canvas, not a few gazing with uninhibited interest at the only white face they may have seen. Ants, mosquitoes, aching hams, feverish note-taking, a wearying incomprehension. One evening I got lost, edging through the unending crowd looking for my students till I gave up. I realised I didn't need to be with them. Any number of children were there, women with babies, rapt villagers. In the day-time I had a shot at writing up what I'd seen as a long poem, that I finished a few days later in Calcutta and called 'The Stage'. Looking back I see how much the audience presence was a part of the event, a truism no doubt to MA students and others, yet it seems worth the saying. For four hours a night the whole village sat in one place, in some sense (as must be true of any audience but never as strikingly to me), a people and a single mind.

The first evening was half taken up with speeches by local politicians and one or two academics, all very vote-friendly it appeared. Then the stage, a red-and-white raised affair of wood and cloth, took over. Tribals – descendants of the indigenous peoples before the Aryans came – danced and leapt, the women moving in a line like the sea, the men whirling with poles. A *madal-*

drummer hurled himself among them all like the wind; then the blank stage. A quintet of ecstatics, followers of the nineteenth-century guru Lalon Fakir, presented his vision (man is one, no god) with song as with every article of their presence. *Ektara* and *dotara* (one-stringed and two-stringed) instruments took over, the players seated in the centre of a circle of women against whom a jester, on the look-out for a bride, surged and wooed in vain, to be rescued at length by a musician turned marriage-broker. A tide of humour held play with a musical and dancing loveliness, haunting in its lightness. A tragic story of a boy lost to a tiger in the Sunderbans jungle, from a troupe of that region, to be saved by friendly crocodile, I remember chiefly for the remarkable acting and singing of the boy himself, who can't have been more than thirteen. His faltering voice as the fear grew real replays itself these fourteen years later. So the first evening ended.

Three stories: 'The Farmer and his Wife', 'The Thief and his Wife', 'The Performer'. The farmer was a lovable idiot, too soft to beat his wife for her bad cooking – the whole field when asked shouted at him to do it – and incapable of the simplest farm duties without getting them wrong. The couple had a dance-step – three back, three forward – that seemed to capture the ordinariness of life and its grace. The thieving couple were good people forced to cross the line with no choice in the matter and no chance of forgiveness: the farce of fate. The performer was another half-wit, who pulverised the crowd with his moronic shyness that flouted all family rules, and with his elastic body that differently broke the norm. Through the lot a background commentary of maracas and trumpet, flute and clarinet, a hint of downtown jazz. Instruments old and new, all now Indian.

The third night saw scenes from the Ramayana. I saw Indrajit killed by Lakshman, Ravana out to avenge the death of his son with Shaktishel the arrow, the appearance of the man-god Ram to save the situation, the loss of his bride Sita to Ravana and her rescue. An old tale of home. I was reminded of scenes from the Mahabharata sculpted on the walls of temples. A story is not words alone. Then a fascinating satirical sequence with a savage political edge. The Prime Minister, in the guise of the god Shiva, is criticised for swanning off to the USA with price-hiking and all forms of corruption rampant at home. In a moment that stands for me between heaven and earth the new South African government was greeted. This in a village field in another continent. The end of apartheid might have had no finer welcome. Finally in a line men spoke and sang a catalogue of horrors, yet less horror in tone than fact: hooligans raping women, jail beatings, murders unattended. The knowing and telling was its own point. The night-dance died.

The last night began with an invocatory song on the loss of trees. Then beautiful dancing women who were in fact men. And a play started up that struck a tiny match-flame in the darkness of Hindu-Muslim mistrust. A poor man's wife has had enough of the two factions she hears are warring at a local festival. Singlehandedly she fires the village to do something. The village administrator, a grave old stick, at first won't listen but in spite of himself drops his reserve. The Hindu and Muslim leaders are confronted, protest loud and long, at last hang their heads in shame and go. A dance of gladness takes over, *holi* powder of the colours of springtime and warmth is scattered, the stage is touched almost by a kiss. Finally a complete riot of a play. A story of moneylenders and a live wire of a corpse, unable to pay up and accidentally convincing wife and son as well as creditors of his terminal inability to do so, had the place in pandemonium. Children were catapulting up all over the field. The creditors give the deceased more money out of fright, coming upon its apparent living ghosthood; they scarper, the family re-unites; and all at once the many disguises of the stage are over. It is to be dismantled the next day. I return to Calcutta.

The students' and their leader's English was good and I was lucky. Over my first year I was to experience more of the swarming power of drama in the open. The autumn festival of Durga Puja, played out over ten days with most of that taken up in a charge of anticipation of the immense ending, told me more deeply of something I can only call an aspect of being alive. So I continued at half pace, going here and there, reading haphazardly and doing a little writing and teaching, but mainly doing not much. Even so I was close to being overwhelmed.

I ndia I have begun to know your stories
    as something closer than a chaotic dream,
a world more present. To pictured furies, glories,
a little more is breathed in, like a stream
inside oneself, beside oneself, a wind
about oneself, within, without, to make
an open country out of pages pinned
in a book-fluttering-by. I am awake
as I walk by your side. But in my head
new pictures I invent, half-stories hear
that never have been told me, never said:
the stream and wind run mocking by and jeer
I am half-deaf, half-blind, half-mad, half-dead.
But no half measures. India you are near.

5

In November of my first year in India, after eight months, I nearly threw it all in. I was ill. A mystery virus left me scarcely able to move. For several days I lay on my bed in my 'cell' in Hotel Maria, dragging slowly up and down Sudder Street when I needed to eat. I'd got to a doctor only to be told it was a mystery. I thought I'd better get back to the UK while I could.

What stopped me was a poem I was writing on Durga Puja, the festival that had just finished. I'd completed about eight of what turned out to be fourteen parts when I found I couldn't walk up the steps from the Metro (Underground) without taking forever. After about a week of the illness and coming to the view I had to go back, I hauled myself into my chair where the poem was still spread on a small table. As I engaged with it for the first time for several days I could feel my body start to improve. I went for a walk the next day by the Hooghly, the stretch of the Ganga River that flows through Calcutta, wondering, wandering, and writing.

I have always been acutely sceptical of all to do with the

spiritual world. It hasn't stopped me entering it in poems, my own or others', for I have long embraced the notion of truth as twofold, poetic and prosaic. Poetic here has the widest range of reference; prosaic is hinged to what one might call dimensional or objective actuality. In the mind of a believer God may be a non-dimensional fact, but (when the chips are down) it'll still be an objective one. From my point of view however the place of the divine is in the poetic landscape. So I'm an atheist but can bring God into a poem, or a goddess. Actually I think everyone's an atheist, which is a prosaic truth-term, and that the categories get mixed; but that's by the way. At any rate the last thing I came to India for was spiritual enlightenment. The Westerners who do this, and have done it, and the line seems to stretch back a century and onward to the crack of doom, are not my cup of *cha*.

And here my Protectress had given me a helping hand. She was Calcutta. I suspended operations on the definitional cut-off point of the realm of the prosaic or poetic and went along, as one does, on both sides of the divide; but with a deeper sense of gratitude.

Of course I knew it was my mind starting to function properly that had given the signals to my body, which had probably been ready to get moving. Later in India I was to deal with various minor ailments, due to age at least as much as to place, and came out of my stay there considerably more aware of the psychosomatic link-up that is always, so to speak, switched on and always to a degree available. But I was beginning to let myself think in a less Western way. Over my time in Calcutta I saw several Westerners, who were there for merely two or three days before hurtling off to Bangkok or Benares, fall ill; and behind the immediate cause, as it seemed, the body was finding a way to let the mind slow down. The river of sensations that is Calcutta is too much to take in for the Westerner new to the country; it needs a traveller's most jealously guarded currency, and the one India is richest in: time.

I used to go up to Canning Street in the north of the city and just stand there in the afternoon. The north is the older part, more densely populated, a seething hive of squashed-up lanes and matchbox shops and howling main roads and everywhere people like an incoming tide. It's also a fairytale from the past, the grand old architecture of the Raj still discernible, if more or less faintly, a chaotic unhurried presence of three hundred years almost whisperingly close. Whereas the south is the new city, more pleasant to live in, but by comparison dull. Still, I chose it to live in when I made a move: less of a headache. But the north was good to stand in at times.

And slowly walk up Canning Street. Hundreds of shops bursting out onto the pavement, a sea of pedestrians not quite blocking the road, bicycles, the occasional private car or yellow taxi edging through, even small lorries. Everything is sold of every colour, shape and size, everyone is there, behind the visible shops are hundreds of others, spaces the size of small offices, or even of cupboards, packing the sides of buildings three or four storeys high. Copper wire or plastic buckets spill out of them; there is a genius in the economical use of small spaces the West has forgotten, if it ever learnt it. Back outside the river returns, the palpable current. At length I walk back to the bus-stand and re-enter the dogged pace and press of the throng. But it's good to be part of it, at times, from outside.

I came to know of a Canning Street rather more real than all this, a place of fire-disaster and disputed political territory (all Calcutta is 'owned', one way or another, by the main parties). A mobster element demanding obedience from all the little shops. But the light side has its reality too. One drank it in, not having to drink too fast.

It was time to leave Sudder Street and commit myself a little more to the business of living in the city. I visited the UK for a month (which I did thenceforth annually if somewhat irregularly) and fixed up for my remaining belongings – books mainly – to be shipped out. Meanwhile I had a room ready to put them in, in Ballygunge in South Calcutta, a busy place, less frenetic than the north, with the beginnings of its own historical personality about it. The room had a separate diminutive kitchen and a bathroom. I returned from England, bought sheets and cutlery and a small fridge and black-and-white television, and in due course picked up my packing-case from the harbour. I felt more of a resident now; and away from Sudder Street, a lot less of an ignorant white tourist. I was learning Bengali and, step by shaky step, learning to live.

Still engaged all too often with the outside of things, I derived a touch of contentment from the easygoing Dhaba restaurant in my new area at the end of the road. It was comparatively cheap and I enjoyed the current of the place, a less dramatic one than the Canning Street avalanche. As soon as you sat down a boy would give you some cold water. They would stretch the rules a little for a regular, giving me coffee sometimes after coffee hours. Whereas the posh Kwality restaurant opposite Dhaba was unimaginative and inflexible. It was the only place round there I could sit and drink a beer so I was often forced to it; but one could hardly relax with one's drink. They had a policy of not sharing tables, and once I invited a couple who were waiting for a table to share mine. Immediately the head waiter was over: not allowed. "I invited them to sit here." "Are you going to pay for their food?" They retired in confusion. Similarly the place would only provide coffee within an impossibly narrow time-frame. The two restaurants came to represent some sort of experiential yardstick, on my pampered learning curve, a true and forced ease: this was Dhaba, that Kwality. Meanwhile there was poverty all around.

I was not to stay long in Ballygunge. The landlord was diabolical. The room had been his library and he refused to move his books, which were both too boring ('Facts on Germany', 'University Regulations') and too unclean to pick up. He was a retired academic, dishonest and bombastic, and had probably always been a petty dictator. But in the few months I was there I (again) settled into the street. Young men occasionally played chess up and down it and invited me to sit at the side of the road and play. It was close, and occasionally I drew, but never quite managed to lose. It was a quiet area and (unlike my landlord) seemed to welcome me into its home.

*H*is books dirty the room. He will not move them.
　　He says, 'I have freed my library for you!'
He writes mean notes, and tells his maid to shove them
anyhow into the room. Only a few
hours a day may I receive a 'phone-call.
He raps out rules. Loud-mouthed, greedy for rent,
he has a conqueror's arrogance. Disdainful
of other viewpoints, he is all-intent
on ruling, over-ruling. Endless headaches
have I, the tenant-subject from the West
of this retired Professor of Aesthetics.
'You are my guest,' he roars, 'my guest, my guest!'
Oh God, I curse the time when some damned Aryan
crossing the hills, gave rise to this barbarian.

6

I was learning a good deal about the language. But not, unfortunately, how to speak it beyond a fairy-cycle stage. Bengali is probably one of the harder Indian languages for the Westerner; but in any case, since my schooldays, when I passed French at GCE but couldn't speak it to save my life, I've cowered behind a monoglot tongue. I was better at reading Bengali (though always in need of guidance the first time through). I got to know quite well how it worked, the grammatical patterns, and came to know several hundred words. Once someone had gone through a poem with me and I'd made my notations I was at ease with it, and could mutter the lines as if they were in my own language. And the extraordinary thing is, so far as the poem was concerned, they were.

As a student of dead languages, long back, I'd been initiated into the translator's dumb art, unlocking the word from the page. It suited me. I was introduced to a short poem by Rabindranath Tagore and was rocked back by it. Another made the situation undeniable: I had a genius on my hands. I translated the two and, sporadically, a number more.

Quite simply, Tagore is the soul of Bengal. A life of eighty years, ending shortly before Independence, did something to bring India into the ever-modern world. By which I mean that Tagore's ideal of citizenship may continue to stand, whatever the situation; and indeed whatever the country: for the man was a true seer. Whatever convolutions India or any land will go through, as I see it Tagore's insight, as that of better-known visionaries, will be relevant.

There's a room in a large house on the Arts campus of Rabindra Bharati Akademi, one of the universities of Calcutta. It's where Tagore was born and died: the university was named after him and built round the family home. I stood silently in the room after reading a translation of his into English of his own Bengali poem; both versions were framed on the wall. The Bengali was beyond me, for the handwriting apart from anything else. I never got to grips with manuscript styles at all and could only ever read the printed word. But the poet's elaborate English hand presented no problem. It was a prose poem (from a rhymed original) and I learnt it as I stood there.

'... In this playhouse of infinite forms I have had my play and here have I caught sight of him that is formless. My whole body and my limbs have thrilled with his touch who is beyond touch; and if the end comes here, let it come – let this be my parting word.'

Feet bare, as in any sanctified spot, in a quiet room with a bed symbolically still, I felt my life join with his. To that extent, at that moment, I became a Bengali. I was later to publish several books of translation of my own of his poems and prose (one of the latter as joint translator). I regard myself as a Tagorean, if an atheist, which he was not. It wasn't his slightly grandiose English prose, though the idea behind it had its effect; but what I already knew of the man, that coalesced in that space of his departure and presence. I shall try to offer the merest suggestion of the individual he was, the shade of a shade.

He was a poet whose creativity naturally flowed over into other areas: not only other forms of writing, short stories, novels, plays, essays and a deal more, not only song-making, choreography, painting; but also into the practical world. He influenced Bengali culture in numerous small ways, from instituting a festival or annual friendship ritual to forward-looking suggestions on language use or clothes wear. He was an educationalist ahead of his time; a far-reaching initiator in village and agricultural development; and a nationalist and internationalist who saw, as clearly as anyone, the directions that needed to be taken for individuality to flourish and the wider community to exist in harmony. He was no mere theoretician or idealist but made things happen: at the same time he was always a poet, exploring, conveying the detail and wonder of existence. He was at once woman and man: for, while unambiguously male, he could fashion woman characters, in his fiction and poetry, who women say and men also feel are women to the core. More significantly his inscape, if one may use the term, indefinably yet unmistakably draws on the power of the two sexes, so that one recognises him with all one's personality. One can go further: for the presence of the man is such that it is not untrue to say that one can feel known by him; that if his life has an essence, it is that of spiritual leader: but poet will do.

He died in 1941. Someone who remembered the event

told me of the shock in the air of the city, that she felt as a ten-year-old child. In the introduction of my first volume of translation of his poems I said, 'To regard his life for a moment as a flow of creative power, it seems to shed a revelatory light on the capacities of the individual,' and I can't better that here.

I was fortunate, then, in having his poems to work on, and friends to help me, as I learnt in my own way to operate in Bengali. At different times I had four or five different language teachers and made little progress in speaking and understanding speech. But I got on much better on the page. The language teachers either bellowed the words at me, intent it seemed to bore through even my carapace of a skull, or were far too nice, treating me with kid gloves instead of testing and re-testing me and making me work. I needed bullying by someone who didn't shout. But slow on the uptake, ageing and refractory, it was a grim proposition I presented. As a teacher I sympathised.

Nevertheless I found I could make myself understood as I went about the city, and taxi-drivers and waiters and so on often were delighted to find someone who had made an effort. Every now and then I lasted into the first few snatches of a conversation; and could hold forth a little if no-one interrupted or smiled at my errors too significantly. And by and large Bengalis have a grace and courtesy in such matters that I miss, back here; as I do so much else. And the poetic discoveries, not only of the original poems but of my – what can I say? – appetite in translating them, gave my venture into the language a fresh edge; at some level, in the word-area, like that of a new existence. But it was not Tagore or his poems that made me stay in the city.

It was part of what had produced Tagore, the poetry in the air. After two weeks of living in Calcutta I had made the decision to stay there, and do no more than visit elsewhere in India; and that was before I had read a single Tagorean word. I knew that the city was a world capital of poetry. So many people were interested in it, could quote reams; they were naturally in touch. The place was not top-heavy on the prosaic side. I was – however much the outsider – invisibly at home.

And at times visibly and audibly. In an electric typewriter shop I found myself talking for two hours with the manager, the sales manager and the accountant round a table. They all loved poetry, loved saying it, wanted to hear English poems, work was suspended, the air danced. At a table in my mind the conversation still goes on. Would there be such a shop in the West?

B lind Fortune scatters
  her coin to the world's end.
A dazzling fountain of the mind,
every street constantly visited
by the sweep and scent of branches
in a fruit-tree's full splendour,
every shed, every room
glittering with pure cascade
of snow-wealth like the air.
What is this miracle of being
owned by richest and poorest
in reckless profusion?
Rain of speech: and here
O Bengal, your sweet words.

7

A good deal happened that first year; and looking back, all I see now is giant *chau* dancers in a mango garden. Magnificently dressed with massive headgear as gods and demons and heroes, as animals and great birds, they parade and somersault and leap to their knees. Again the whole village is there and mythic episodes have taken over. Except for the youngest of the children (and myself), all are in touch with events; and the freshness to the telling of old tales is like an evening wind. I am in Purulia, a rural district of West Bengal, to see the performance of one of the oldest survivals of indigenous dance. Earlier on in the day I asked what time it would start. I was met by incomprehension and a sweep of the arm that took in the village. "When they go."

Such freshness for me, too, lay beneath the dust of Calcutta; though it could be hard going, living there, and not only for the newcomer. "Nothing is easy in Calcutta," I was told by someone born and bred in the place, and it could be the city motto. Yet as an image of the India that I met, or that met me, early on, the masks in the mango garden speak a silent message, the cavorting forms, and the scores of children's faces at the side.

It was a festival of two or three days, and of a further art-form, *nachni* dancing. A *nachni* is a dancing mistress, not in the sense of teacher, someone from a low caste attached to the household of a *rasik* or male musician. (Caste discrimination is officially outlawed but it is ingrained in the character of the land, a fact of life and death.) The *nachni* contributes her earnings to the *rasik* and his family but is treated literally like dirt, an unclean presence to be shunned outside the occasion of her singing and dancing. In death her body is abandoned in the forest or unceremoniously slung into the river, legs tied together. Her songs are in the *jhumur* tradition and of a searing, haunting beauty. I saw the dancing of several *nachni* and heard their singing. I do not think it is wrong to say they are servants of their art. At any rate when they perform it is with an infectious happiness. There was a master *rasik* at the finale of the festival who beckoned one after another of the *nachni* to dance with him. He was a thin old man whose minimalist dance-steps bespoke a pure musical authority. Each *nachni* was delighted and humbled to be his partner. I left Purulia, I think, with less desire to understand in a cut-and-dried way, and perhaps the sense of a dim ray having lightly brushed a lazy inner eye. More asleep, more awake.

Before I left, an eye-popping moment of another kind altogether. I had walked out into a field behind where I was staying, intrigued by a rise in its centre. I walked up it far enough to see over the top and have never reversed direction as fast or stored as much in a blink. The rise concealed a dip with a large pond where scores of women and girls were bathing naked. Thank God I wasn't seen; at least no accusation came my way of peeping. And thank God, while I'm at it, for the glimpse. It's not a bad inner photo to have.

I wrote a short poem on the *chau* dance and the *jhumur* singing that was published in the magazine festival issue of 'The Statesman' newspaper. It was from this newspaper, incidentally, that the English periodical took its name. The magazine comes out every year in the autumn as part of the celebrations of Durga Puja and I contributed annually thenceforth. I had been told of a publisher, P.Lal, who was interested in writing in English, and approached him with a collection of poems: after a year I had a book's worth. Not only did he accept, but in conversation he discovered that I had been little published in England, and he offered to bring out all my poetry in a succession of volumes. His productions, Writers Workshop books, were a joy to behold and to hold; his own calligraphy adding a touch of individuality and distinction to each sari-cloth-covered volume. It was a semi-vanity press set-up, but an author had merely to spend a small sum on a number of copies for himself, and the production was outstandingly fine. Suddenly thirty years of writing was to move out of a jumbled carrier bag into books.

He told me to sort out what I'd got and let him know how many volumes it might make, and I spent a strange fortnight on an archaeological dig through thousands of scraps of paper. It came to eleven books pre-India that he published over the next few years together with several more written there. After all this time my poems had a lifeline.

I was to spend many hours going over proofs, hand-set, hand-printed, in the mosquito-haunted sitting-room of his printer, and occasionally in the shed outside where a couple of men with no English except a wayward letter-recognition set the pages, character by individual metal character, in their lines in rows on trays. 'In a lap-top, push-button age Writers Workshop prefers Gutenberg-style printing,' proclaims P.Lal in his flowing italic script in a 1998 volume; though he acceded to the electronic media later. His books are still as beautiful as ever. He started Writers Workshop fifty years ago as I write, in 1958, and nearing eighty himself, is an Indian institution. His translation into poetic prose and verse of the Mahabharata epic will come to be seen as significant in the course of English literature. His many other translations from the Sanskrit also are notable for their deftness and ease. His own poetry may be the finest in English from an Indian man; though there are two or three women to steal the laurels. He is known as a university teacher far and wide with great affection and respect. Nothing is ever too much trouble; and he keeps his word. A gifted man and a good one.

In my latter years in Calcutta I lived not so far away and sometimes he would send round a pizza he had made. The gesture he made of commitment to my writing (in which he can have done no more than break even) changed my life somewhat; while the pizza lent a variety to the menu of the day. But together they sum up P.Lal for me as someone I am fortunate to know.

Needing to move from the Ballygunge apartment I found a ground-floor flat in Park Street. The landlord lived in a separate flat in a nearby building. The interview was interesting. "Mr Winter, if you live here you won't have any women to stay of course." "Then I won't be living here." "Well ... who would be staying?" "Maybe a friend from England, I don't know." "But would an Indian woman be staying?" "Maybe, I don't know." "But would many Indian women be staying?" I saw his problem. "Mr Puri, I'm fifty-two years old. No-one is going to tell me who can stay with me and who can't. If it's any relief to you I don't intend to have a string of Park Street prostitutes coming in and out." He was mollified and we signed the contract. I had met an American in Ballygunge who fitted the Western male stereotype only too easily, paying the police to find him under-age girls. Mr Puri proved to be an agreeable and uninterfering landlord. I was in a studio flat on the most vibrant street in Calcutta, ten minutes' walk from my beloved Fairlawn garden in Sudder Street. I was writing book reviews for 'The Statesman', my poetry was being printed. Things were looking up.

*L*ady as if from out of the hand of April
a peril of beauty came, shining the land
that once was rootless, bare ... what have you found me?
What is this field of tall strange brilliant flowers?
This shade-inviting red-blossomed tree? This patch
as wide as a far life-time, of tender grass?
Lady I am the land holding these riches
and all is new. No drought, nor other danger
can reach this island of self-growth. For lady
you have allowed my own word to that free water
which is the eyes and hearing of all. Calcutta
you have published my books. Yet there is the peril
each altering moment, of death. But death is a nothing.
For in an April hand my word will not die.

8

I would like to give an idea of the setting of my new home. A precinct of several large-roomed buildings with a fair amount of open space set back from the main road, at the same time it housed the sheltered-rich and the dirt-poor. The latter looked after the former and lived in hovels dotted about the estate. They were for the most part related, family members finding openings for kin in the hallowed Indian tradition, or simply floor-space. There must have been twenty-five or thirty of them at any one time, and about fifteen flats, some with their own live-in servants. The flat-dwellers for the most part barricaded themselves behind extra locked gates and lived as if the others did not exist, except as part of the economic equation; yet the distance between the two also held an unsignalled neighbourliness. The poor knew the secrets of the rich. And the children of one group played with those of the other.

Above me at the top lived a dealer in ceramic antiques, with rooms full of great porcelain jars and the like. It was reckoned to be one of the rarer private collections in the land. He had a son in his early twenties, an urbane fellow of powerful build, who was mugged one evening in the precinct grounds by two of the less neighbourly of the hovel-dwellers. Below him a couple lived with a son of limited ability. The mother (who was from middle Europe) was often to be seen leading him through the grounds, an obese young man with the high-pitched querulous voice of a child. Then there was an ancient Anglo-Indian, a hockey player, musician and photographer of repute, with a fairytale album of snaps of old Calcutta. A heart surgeon lived next door to me and businessmen and their families were settled here and there. An art gallery lay at one corner. A half-mad man of middle age, scarcely even a hovel-dweller, used to sit out on a concrete strip and sleep there much of the time, attended by a touchingly faithful woman. His stare made one uncomfortable as one passed him on the way out to Park Street. A young woman in her mid-twenties used to clean my flat on a Saturday morning, sometimes accompanied by her eldest daughter who was eleven or twelve and to whom I'd give five rupees when I paid her mother. She kept the little blue notes to buy her mother a present. She was due to be married off in a year or two. There was a youth of an engaging friendliness who would steal anything left outside. An acquaintance of his lived on and off site, a darker character entirely.

The two of them knocked on my door one evening and demanded money. R. was with me, a Bengali lady who had often stayed and whom I was later to marry. We refused, and the sinister one threatened violence. His face had a disturbing pathological twist, and I knew he'd been in prison though not the details. He didn't carry too much conviction however and he and his sidekick let themselves be drawn into a discussion of the whole business. When I reminded him that the police station was next door he laughed and looked quite sane for a moment. "They won't touch me. I'm Congress!" He was referring to the Congress political party which had its tentacles everywhere that the major party in the state, the Communist Party of India (Marxist) or CPI(M), and a new party, Trinamool ("Grass Roots") didn't. Eventually the two came out with what they thought was the clincher. "We'll tell Mr Puri (the landlord) an Indian woman is staying here." I asked him to go and do so. Finally they left, but for some time after that at night the bell would be rung: we didn't answer. I was nervous for a week or two as I went into the narrow dark passage leading into and out of the precinct, but after a time stopped worrying. Nothing happened.

R. was a petite lady with a smile that could crack a mountain. She worked with an NGO that she had founded with her father about fifteen years before, that was dedicated to community development, in village areas for the most part but also in Calcutta itself. Its method was cultural rather than directly economic, the aim being to increase awareness of approaches to take and options to adopt and issues to consider, in places where tradition ruled and discussion that questioned it was ruled out. Its means of engagement was by the use of art-form, puppetry, drama, song, in some cases adapting local variants. Thus it was I found myself on stage in a village outside Calcutta frantic to spot my cue.

Her group had given me a part of four separate lines in a short play about the greed and possessiveness – of such groups as their own. Non-governmental organisations are funded by charitable foundations from abroad or by the Indian government itself, whether state or central. In any case some of them are rackets. So this play amusingly showed an NGO descending on a village and exploring the possibilities of power: a smart office here, a claim for extra funds there, hierarchy squabbles and so on. It ended in a vivid tug-of-war, played out almost as a dance, the villagers on one end of the rope, the urban careerists the other. There was an appreciative murmur from the actual villagers and the odd exclamation; but not at one point. Since I couldn't follow the Bengali except in flashes, as each line of mine came up I had an extra cue: the cast all looked at me. The audience must have found it hilarious, but were very polite; in any case, pinned in the headlights as it were, I managed to forget one of my lines. A sympathetic silence filled the hall, deafening for a few beats. The play went on.

But what happened after it was far more memorable. There was an impromptu hour-long debate between cast and audience. The play had made use of a couple of well-known Hindi love songs, fitting new words to the melodies. To most of the audience it was an unacceptable hijacking. It was a fascinating discussion. (I was kept in touch with it and invited to contribute.) To the town-dwellers a satirical lyric was valid in terms of art. To the villagers it was aesthetically wrong. These were love songs, the tune indivisible from the words. There seemed to be a distance of a hundred years between the two sides though it was only an hour's drive. And I think there was.

R. and I had a nervous start to our nearness. Her English was good, my Bengali laughable, but there were wider gulfs, of age, of background. Neither of us really knew what we wanted either. After a long stint as paterfamilias I had spun free and more or less adjusted to living alone. She had had an agony of a marriage and was separated and in the throes of a divorce (that was to go on for years). She had a daughter, P., six years old when I first met them. We played Snakes and Ladders and P. and I had a disagreement about the rules. It's thirteen years ago as I write and that was probably our worst argument. R. used to come round to my Park Street flat on Wednesday evenings and make *kichuri*. It's a dish of rice and *dal*, *ghee*, maybe some vegetables, and R. would add an omelette. It's often cooked when the rain is falling, but I wolfed it at any time. A tradition began of a few friends coming round on the same evening, mostly Bengalis and also the occasional visitor I met; and poetry and song and conversation gave me my first homegrown ingredient in the Bengali recipe for living.

*I*think a country shares its name like children
can share a special name or word. It ties
them in a secret. How can I, a foreigner
be felt as of your land, under your skies?
I cannot find the knack to keep you company.
There can be no familiar surprise
of known and knowing. Through a screened-off history
I cannot tell the story of your eyes.
And I am twenty years more aged than you.
I travel down: while you are in your glory.
The land of time and land of space both reckon
that we can never be as close as children.
Our distant worlds impose their separate view.
But eyes of love inform a different story.

9

In a civilised society where togetherness is taken for granted, *adda* is a fact of existence. The d's are separate: *ad-da*; and it means, quite simply, that special everyday occasion when people are together for a talk. There is no topic as such, a poem may be recited, a song sung, or it may be mere gossip; yet the Western equivalent of 'chewing the fat' lacks the sense of privilege in talking with another or others, that is an Indian's birthright. Circles of acquaintances gather in tea-houses all over the city at certain times in the week, one may belong to five or six such; or it may be a parent and child sitting together on a bed in the evening, as R. and P. were wont to do in their small flat, telling stories, chatting, and again, maybe learning or swapping a song or poem or two. Nor is it any different in the village. To be with another or with others is valued, and in a way honoured by the presence of song – whether it is sung or spoken or silent.

Of course this is an outsider's pontificating: to a Bengali *adda* is, there's a word for it, no more need be said. I used to sit in India Coffee House on College Street in a gale of talk that rose and fell from about fifty small tables, glance at a book purchased from the forest of book-stalls in the street, and savour the crashing of the wind. A large 'SILENCE PLEASE' notice on the wall made its own unheard comment. Years later on a visit one afternoon I sensed something missing. It took me a while to spot the notice had gone. In a way the place was not so different from a large saloon bar that I used to sit in, The Bull in Streatham, where at a certain table you could listen in to a conversation at a table the other side of the great throng. The sound reflected off the ceiling at the right angle, but it was always a desultory conversation for some reason; and within the slightly subdued atmosphere of the place, one was driven to sit elsewhere. The general talk in the Coffee House was no doubt of such diurnal matters, and there wouldn't be much singing or reciting in a packed venue like that; yet the place carried a charge. While most tables would have their two or three in an afternoon chat, many would be swamped by a ring of habitués; the same the world over of course; but this was a place where one came to talk, to listen, what one sipped was incidental. Like the trains, I felt at some dim level, like the roads that were not roads but rivers of pedestrians, these were venues of the gods. A current swept through the great building; one felt it as one went up the stone steps and turned right, away from the quiet book show-rooms in the corridor to the left, into the mêlée. To use the word with a touch of the original sense of possession by the divine, to me the India Coffee House, in its old poky spaciousness, was a house of enthusiasm.

Outside a flotilla of second-hand book-stalls idled in

the sun. One of the main universities of Calcutta is in College Street and plenty of students are always there, picking through the miscellaneous piles; but as with the Calcutta Book Fair, of which more later, it's by no means a preserve of the well-schooled or the well-heeled; there's no sense of cut-off. It's a place of the people. Once I sauntered down the street making a note of unlikely companions: Aristotle's 'Physics' wedged between 'Oliver Twist' and 'The Three Musketeers'; 'Orthopaedics' weighing down 'Everyone's Book of Classic Cars'. The stall-owners, who run an intelligence system behind the scenes of customer need and supply, gave me up that afternoon as a bad job.

In India everything is linked. A personal closeness, the counterpart of the West's newly unearthed sense of alienation, is breathed in and out. Mirroring the informal institution of *adda*, a momentary rite of Spring brings the individual and the season together, touching on the tie between family and friends with a delightful freshness. *Holi* is the daubing of loved ones with coloured powders, a scattering of colour, a blooming of green and yellow and red and other hues on face and hair and arms, a flash of renewal. It can get out of hand. It so happened that the festival fell on the first day of my stay in the country. I was advised by residents of the Baptist guest-house to stay indoors: "Children throw paint at foreigners, they're wild, it's dangerous." But I had to go out to my day of welcome. Dollops of paint tipped from upstairs windows onto the pavement narrowly missed me a few times; and then there was indeed a horde of children threatening with cans of paint and wild eyes. I was later told they may well have been up all night and on *ganja*. A relaxed dismissive schoolmasterly handling of the situation failed to make any impression at all: and I was rescued by a gentleman who bellowed them out of range and pointed me towards a Muslim area nearby. These streets were safe; it was a Hindu custom.

I returned to the guest-house with the trophy of a little paint on my clothes and skin and not sorry to have ventured out. In later years the *holi* morning was a precious greeting among the members of my family on the balcony of our flat. But the best celebration of the event was at one of the estates in Salt Lake, a massive housing development area on the north-eastern side of the city, where R. and P. lived before coming to share with me. After daubing one another we went out to the general throng and spent the rest of the morning lining up at this door and that to anoint and be anointed, the celebrations crowned for me with a bucket of water unexpectedly emptied over my head. Later that day I took a taxi back to the city centre looking like something on fire; no notice was taken, there were many such. A long time before, a Jewish baby, I had gone through the circumcision ritual and later, adopted by a Gentile couple, had experienced a formally-Christian schooling very much from the outside, unbaptised and unconfirmed. On an entirely human level, all gods out of sight and out of mind, as I look back now I see the bucket of water as a Hindu baptism.

The monsoon lashed down on the ground outside the door of the Park Street apartment. It was my second year in the city. As I watched the rain it was the simple things that sprang to mind, in two villages where I had friends, as well as in the city itself. It strikes me that I've said little about getting to know people. It wasn't as easy as it may have appeared and it took a toll; there were misunderstandings and unreal expectations on either side; and yet I felt known by many. And also by places. *ami Kolkatar jamai*, I would say sometimes to general approval, *I'm Calcutta's son-in-law*. I was a new enough addition to the household and the family was an unknown quantity. But for some reason, whenever the monsoon tore down and took over the background, I was at home.

L ady while the rain beat there was this:
   a laughing holi procession at Salt Lake City
a rapids of goods and people on Canning Street
a twilit flow at the Ballygunj 'Dhaba' restaurant
a crows-and-car-beep duet in the Fairlawn garden
the watchful banyan-tree of Badkulla village
past Chakdaha town a breathing forest-green
a roads-and-pavement Trade Fair at Gariahat Market
a train-seat thankfully free at Sealdah Station
a quiet back-street cycle-rickshaw at Tollygunj
an ocean-wind in the talk at India Coffee House
the silent tree-crowds of the Botanical Garden
the old-and-new of and around Calcutta ...
all this as the rain beat on the hard ground.

10

I was introduced to an academic whose family showed me great hospitality. For about a year I went round on Thursday mornings for breakfast. I used to talk for a few moments on arrival with the professor's father, an octogenarian, in his sitting-room on the ground floor, after which we made our way two floors up to join the family. He was always up early and I started arriving a little earlier for the conversation. Soon we regularly spent an hour before the meal as he told me of his life.

Mr Roy had lived in the house all his life and the road itself was named after an illustrious forebear. He was a retired military man with a neatness typical of such; and a love of poetry and a restless driven soul to which the background seemed fortuitous. But he was not a whit at odds; but in a finely-contained universe where opposites raged in calm. I have not known a person more at home in himself. His account included the military and much else. I am still coming to terms with the scope of it.

He grew up in an extended family. His father had elder brothers and the generations lived together in a large, somewhat hierarchical household, three houses then as one side-by-side. Early on he understood the need for rules and had an inkling of the freedom to be found in their acceptance. Murders committed by fighters in the Independence movement were part of his boyhood; he recalled them with a kind of amusement. He started boxing in his teens, a sport frowned upon by the family though his father looked the other way. When there was no disguising a blow to the nose one of his father's elder brothers instructed him to stop. He stopped: telling me with satisfaction, "No discussion then. The elders were in command." And took up photography, which he revelled in, taking a prize in an international competition judged in the Berlin of 1936 for a snap from the ground of his father on a balcony, with a cloud he had waited twenty minutes for. His first job was in films, Bombay Talkies, camera-man in a prestigious outfit. But his mother disapproved of the company she imagined he might keep: film actresses imitating American stars. He was desperate to stay but obeyed her. With no clear path in view he applied to the Indian army for a commission and was accepted.

The army was run by the British then as was the national apparatus. When I first went to secondary school half the atlas (it may have been a touch out-of-date) was coloured red to denote the British Empire. One good thing staying in India did for me was, however belatedly, to stamp out any dim half-sense that one land can ever belong to another. Ironically enough Mr Roy was an admirer of the British. It is not so unusual in someone of his generation. As a boy he had taught himself to trace the shires of England on a map in the mind. He loved English poetry and reckoned that at one time he'd had half 'The Golden Treasury' by heart. He respected the professionalism of the British command ("Brigadier Jack Peterson liked my boxing") and soon became an officer himself, rising as high as an Indian could at the time. After Independence he stayed in the army many years as an Intelligence Officer: it was his main career. Another germinated and grew up alongside, a parallel commitment. He became an astrologer.

In the Second World War he spent three years in the Fourteenth Army in the jungle on the edge of Burma, patrolling and fighting shadows for the most part, but with moments of savage engagement. "We would not allow the Japanese an inch of India." One night, on the look-out for someone rumoured to spy for the Japanese, he slept in a pagoda and woke at the approach of a tall bearded man who asked him in English, "Why have you come here?" Instinctively answering in English with the beginnings of a concocted story he was cut short: *apni-to bangali?* Are you Bengali? Mr Roy too recognised the accent in the other and they talked through the night. His first thought, lying on the pagoda floor, had been that his target had turned up and was going to kill him. He was right on the first count; as to the second, anything may have happened. Instead there was an informing moment. The man's wife had died in childbirth and he had sold his business in Rangoon to pay for his daughter's upkeep in an ashram, and given himself to welfare work, going from village to village (and so arousing suspicion on the Allied side). He had insight into Mr Roy's life, including things that had not happened yet (a wounded eye, a bleeding foot), and something more like a shape of things to come.

According to Mr Roy it all came about; and though for now he had merely a prediction as to himself, he had also a certainty from the long conversation that there was more behind events than he had dreamt of. He set out to investigate further.

After the War he was stationed for three years in Madras and in his spare time learnt much from an aged gentleman who instructed him never to set down his knowledge in a book; and who himself on occasion would consult an ancient manuscript. As musicians know the guru-pupil tie is a sacred one. I sensed it at a distance here and later was to learn of it a little more directly. When I met Mr Roy he practised the art of astrology both by post, people sending him their date and place of birth and he replying with the horoscope, and in an everyday way, someone in the know. Once someone passed the window and called in something through the open bars that I didn't catch. Mr Roy called back "Budhbar" and the man went on by. "What was Wednesday the answer to?" I asked. "Oh, he's applying for a job and wanted to know the best day to send the letter." I carried on listening to the account of a colourful life.

He returned to camerawork when he left the Army, shooting film for CBS of New York; he also ran a photographic studio, and worked for the German steel firm Siemens. He was based always in Calcutta and died there shortly before I left. I have said next to nothing here but – it will not surprise the reader – wrote a long poem on his life. He gave his permission and let me tape the whole long rambling account: I used to listen to it in my flat in Park Street, playing parts over and over again as he spoke with a certain susurration that made some words hard to catch. I realised later I may have moved a little closer to the personality behind the words, tuning in to the tonal pattern. One thing I remember above all is the way he said poetry. He half sang, half recited it, English or especially of course Bengali, inspired.

I have never imagined there was anything in astrology but for the sake of understanding him and entering the plot, so to speak, suspended my disbelief. It was something that seemed to happen now and then in various contexts and perhaps in India as a whole. Again, looking back, I see someone freed a smidgen from his Western mental harness. It is almost with regret that I know I cannot do that again; but more, I am grateful that for a time it could be so.

A geometry is practised on my soul
  that cuts in quadrants and down parallel lines
a kind of sketch-map. From before birth, it seems
an instrument of fracturing strength has plotted
a chart that never stops. Now for the time
adopted and held close to India's side,
I seem to see a fragmentary truth.
I half-glimpse areas and repeating patterns –
and then whatever is shown is slid away.
I do not wish to see. But now Creation
is manic on my life. I am in its hand
and almost feel its murderous, life-giving fingers
break and make. But now this land has lifted
and put in safe, the deepest piece of me.

11

For a time I taught an evening a week in a non-formal school. Any number of middle-class Calcuttans give some free time to such an enterprise: it is often teaching kids in a *bustee* (slum area); but a doctor may give free medical advice, for example. There is quite a tradition of interaction between the haves and the have-nots on such a level. A *bustee* is more compressed than the term 'slum area' suggests. Once I was taken round a building inhabited by about two thousand five hundred people. Some corridors were ghastly but most were clean, with a couple of children at one point doing homework, escaping the room-throng. I passed a few makeshift shops. I was taken into room after room and came out after an hour shattered by the sheer numbers: many small rooms had twenty or so in them, it went on and on and on, a subterranean effect though the building stood quite high. At one point in a corridor I passed a man attended by two of his family who was dying of TB. There seemed to be no question of his being taken to hospital. The whole place largely ran itself without interference from outside agencies. I staggered into the street certain I'd rather sleep outside in the open than inside. Fortunately I didn't have to do either. At another level the visit was a sombre reminder of the scope for human adjustment.

Where I taught the set-up was more of a shanty town, a maze of separate small homes. About twenty children would come to the community social room which was left free for the occasion. The first time I was taken by an academic who had instituted the class – that's all the "school" was there, a weekly class. The children asked me questions through him. They were on the lines of whether I was married and the number of children I had; then a boy of about eleven, dressed in scruffy clothes too big for him, asked a longer question my friend laughed at before translating. What difficulties had I had to deal with coming on my own to a strange city? I answered briefly about not understanding a lot of things and being lonely sometimes: he understood. He was scarily bright; but I saw little of him. He turned up to a couple of classes I took on my own, in which they taught me more Bengali than I taught English. But his background was all over the place and so was he. A small thick snake came through a hole in the wall one session to hysterical excitement and disappeared quickly enough. The children were not so different from those I teach at present at a fee-paying public school in England. But the forces that drove them were.

They were wonderfully polite one evening when haltingly I told them of something idiotically foolish I'd done on the way to the class. I gaze at my fingers typing these words as I recall it. It could all be gone. I took a short cut over a double railway line. It was dark (as it always is from early evening) and with my not properly observing where I was stepping my shoe lodged in some kind of junction between two rails and stuck. As I tried to wriggle it free the lights of a train approached. I was carrying quite a large bag which made bending down to untie the lace awkward and so I carried on jerking my foot. The shoe freed itself and I made the platform, hearing people start to exclaim and shout. I counted the seconds till the train thundered past. Four. I told my students on arrival, mainly in mime to cover the vocabulary gap, and ended *ami khub boka, khub khub boka*. I'm very stupid, very very stupid. No Sir, no Mr Joe, not stupid, no no. They were shocked I should say so. We carried on, singing 'Ten Green Bottles' if I remember rightly.

Occasionally one saw a disturbing maturity in a child in such a set-up, as for example when I found myself teaching Noughts and Crosses to two girls of ten or eleven. One was just that, a mere girl, the other was a little woman, by which I mean there was an aura to her of being sexually aware and experienced. She did not flirt; but one sensed a knowledge in her of dealing with men, and of coping with the knowledge: she was not distressed but a little more capable or powerful as it seemed; though I may have been quite wrong about it all. She was quick enough to pick up Noughts and Crosses, and it was refreshing to see her childish delight as she won a game.

The slums of Calcutta can be a dark world. I heard of the story of a very beautiful teenage girl who was guarded at night by older women to protect her from rape, but to no avail. And (it goes without saying) a world of loving care and concerns. R.'s sister taught in a day-time non-formal school that I visited. I was astonished to see two five-year-old girls each looking after a baby of one or two. They did so with an unfussy practicality, one handing over her charge to the other while she excused herself for a minute for example, both seeming to know exactly what to do. The babies were at ease and in no danger. The mothers were at work. The city authorities would sometimes take an interest, not in the people but the space they occupied, clearing an area of makeshift dwellings without warning. They would reconstruct and resettle a little way along. My class came to an end fairly soon. I count it a privilege in my teaching life. In Britain we say "Education, Education, Education". In Calcutta, on her special day, people pay their respects to Saraswati, and celebrate her presence among them.

She is the goddess of learning and poetry and music and song. On her day in West Bengal, sometime in January or early February, there will be an image of her in makeshift temples (*pandals*) everywhere in village and town, and of the swan she is said to arrive on; there will be a lotus next to her and also a book or two, maybe a dictionary, while a priest utters prayers in Sanskrit and the crowd repeats the responses. Wealthy homes will have their own service in-house; otherwise it is a public matter, where the community in more or less every street is the family and the goddess everyone's dear guest. The crowd will throw flowers and leaves (the *anjali*-offering) during the ritual and after it will share in the sweets (*prasad*) that they have also set at the image's foot. Later there will be a feast (*bhog*) in her honour. Since becoming acquainted with Saraswati my life has been richer. I cannot imagine Hindu belief ever being vitiated by theological arguments of ontology and transubstantiation. If it is it will be Hinduism no longer.

I am no Hindu but glad to have been warmed by a closeness for a time. Once in a village I saw a small hut in a field next to a school. Nothing else was in the field. I asked what the hut was for. It was where small girls and boys went alone to say a prayer to Saraswati before their first reading lesson. It is one of the simplest and most moving memories I take with me from India. I have been reading for over sixty years now and am more than content to imagine a visit to that hut at the start of it all.

*C*old, struggling with words, I heard a voice
   that spoke the sense of poetry in a room
where student dryness fed an internal gloom.
It was my twentieth year. And then no choice:
the goddess sang to me, and the day changed
and took on strength, and light broke through, and sang
of me to her. And though a death-wind sprang
it could not hold: and I was not estranged.
Then all my life has known a timeless river
of flame, of song, of love's delight, of praise
for her whose day is guardian to my days,
for her whose voice includes my voice for ever.
Today we meet. It is her name I say
in India on Saraswati's day.

12

I have been standing for an hour at the edge of a platform in a station in the countryside waiting for a train. I am at the edge to stop the ring of onlookers circling me completely. They stand and look, I stand and am looked at, it's late, I'm tired, there's about thirty of them, men and youths, no-one says anything. Some of them won't have seen a white person before. My Bengali isn't good enough to ease the situation, nor do I feel like trying. I just wait. In the train it's not so bad.

Mostly it's different. I buy vegetables from a market and sense a delight in the stall-holder that I can say what's necessary. Or a taxi-driver tells me I'm the first white fare in ten years he can talk with. That surprises me as there are a handful of European women in Calcutta, usually widows or divorcees of Bengali men, who are fluent; almost no European men though. In the town I'm not a curiosity and I have something to do and a few words I can find to go with it. But this is the countryside and I'm not doing anything but waiting. If I try a little basic conversation the attention will increase exponentially. I stay quiet.

I've lived as an adult in London and, like a townee, holidayed in the country. But my childhood was spent in the village (Cornwall, Buckinghamshire) and my old age may be. The village bond is irreplaceable. On the other hand the parochialism is unbearable. My teenage judgement of the issue had stayed more or less frozen in time, and come to mean less and less. In India the first part of it came alive again.

Despite a little awkwardness travelling out and back, and a little discomfort staying there, my trips to this or that village in West Bengal were reassuring as to something in me I did not know I – or anyone really – still had. They took me back, far back, past my childhood, to an older time. For all the caste structure and the superstition, the closed circle of thought that is part of a village, for all the nearness of the horizon, the horizon opened. Mawkish as it is to say so, there is a capacity in us for living simply, and for neighbourliness, that economic progress is slowly but surely dulling. One is what one is; but what one is not can be validated too.

Large numbers of the urban middle class have a village they go back to at regular intervals, where a part of the family still resides. On the other hand large numbers are squeamish about staying overnight in such a place and are cutting roots; again, there is an academic interest in the village that earns a doctorate and increases the distance. I am thankful for the freshness knowing and visiting a few people in the rural tradition in India has brought me; and find in England I draw on it to an unexpected extent. I may be wrong about it all but merely the opportunity to think about the issue has been welcome.

Occasionally one would come across a villager in difficulties in the metropolis. On a platform in the Metro I saw a middle-aged man collapsed in tears. A few people were reassuring him. He had lost his wife somewhere on a Metro train. Everyone was telling him to go to a police station but he seemed not to have the faintest idea: for him she was gone. In passing I recall another time I saw a man weeping bitterly: a car had driven into a cycle-rickshaw and smashed it, and the rickshaw-*wallah*, uninjured, was weeping as if his heart would break. (No exchange of insurance details there.) Coming back to the Metro, two or three times I witnessed the bemused attempts, once of a whole family, to step onto the escalator. Of course most country people coped quickly enough; for after all, Calcutta absorbs many hundreds a month to live on the streets or otherwise make do. But one way or another one is always aware at some level of the city/country conflux and contrast. It's in the air.

Calcutta itself can seem like a massive village, with beggars on the steps on the High Court for example – a spot from which in Delhi or Mumbai, it goes without saying, they will be swept away. Calcutta does not have the self-consciousness of a city; it ambles, it does not march; the look on its face is an easygoing one, open without being sincere. Whereas other more forward-looking places will try to present an earnest demeanour but it will be one with something to hide. (Not only in India I may add.) I admit a prejudice here, a parochial outlook even. I belong nowhere but unlike Wimbledon, say, where I lived for longer, Calcutta did not seem averse to the dust of my soul.

One character I met for a few seconds early on stays in my

head, irrationally no doubt, as person and place in one: an
impetuous spirit. I had been on a television programme for
a local station, 'Our Friend' or somesuch, that interviewed
visitors to the city. I told a silly story about not being able
to decipher a slogan in a bus, and read out one or two
poem-translations; and a few days later a small man ran
up to me at a street corner, talked about the programme,
thrust a street map of Calcutta into my hands, refused to
accept payment and dashed off. He sold the little map-
booklets for a living. I have it in front of me now, a minute
hundred-page directory. I used it often; but having it has
also given me direction, and still does, though I could
not say how. One lives by signs maybe, to a degree; at all
events they can store the odd stray spot of understanding
that has gathered, and that needs no elucidation.

Rambling on (or ambling) I'll re-tell the bus story. It was
before I'd learnt the Bengali letters. There was a slogan
of two words in a bus above the window in a flowing
script, the first word short, the other thrice as long. To
make conversation with the gentleman wedged next to
me I pointed at it and said: "No Smoking?" He looked
at it, looked at me incredulously and told his companion
who told others. Everyone was howling with laughter.
Someone told the driver and the bus was rocking too.
There must have been a hundred people on the single-
decker. Everyone knew the English "No Smoking". No-
one would tell me what the words said. Finally I was put
out of my misery: it was "Ma Sitala", who is a mother
goddess who defends against disaster: but not me.

Sometimes writing has to work its way around the edges.
At any rate it is time to enter a moment that took me back

and on and outside the usual start and close to things. I was at a village called Kaluhar in Purulia District that electricity had not yet reached. Everyone sat outside into the night and at last we ate at long tables under the stars. I found myself writing the poem below. I had to get it down. I was eating with my fingers, of the right hand as always, and unable to write with my left was forced to put my food down, fish the pen out and write. As I carried on eating I carried on writing. There was a sense of mild horror at the table but also of understanding. Despite our restaurant culture there is more of a food aesthetic in India than here and my offence was the greater, as the *dal* and rice and vegetables graced the pen and paper and the words splodged in among the food. But there was something I had to sift out from the night about me.

Lady there are horned shadows of cows on the mud walls
in this night village. By a kerosene lamp
flickers a family's unhurried conversation.
A stray dog plunders the dust. A house away
a man is singing to children. What will happen
to a night-closeness, lady, when television
leaks through the air? When the power line is cut off
by a lurid electric glare? Now an idle traveller
has found a home he knew before he was born.
What strangeness, now, what peace. Above us the stars
startle, lady, with their old news. Down here
I am not alone. Soon I will be returned
from a larger world. But in a certain night village
beyond even India, tonight I live beyond death.

13

Into my studio flat in Park Street, through one barred window and out another, a wasp would sometimes drift, voluminously clad in yellow, a little silk parachute. They did not seem to mind me and awarded the room the honour of building a nest directly outside one of the windows, beneath an overhanging projection. I would stand on a small stool just this side of the window, staying still, many minutes at a time, watching the process. On a level with my face, a foot or two away the other side of the open bars, they circled about, ever so slowly constructing a home out of a bodily secretion. I refused to let anyone interfere with the nest, though my cleaner was horrified. She told me of a dead man she'd seen on a platform of Sealdah Station covered by a mass of the same insects. I let them be, the nest was finished, and for several weeks I co-existed with my new neighbours, with no harm to either side. But I went away for a month to England and in my absence they were smoked out, I think. The nest hung empty for a couple of years and I forgot to take it when I moved. I came for it the day after and it was gone.

The people next door who had taken over the flat for their undergraduate son said they knew nothing of it but I think they did. It would have been a fine memento of my time there but I find it hangs in my mind as it did outside the window, and brings back the summer there.

I had other, less welcome neighbours, with rather more direct notions as to how to share a residence. *Ui poka* (white ants) devoured half a curtain during one of my absences. In the same month they also ate a significant part of the wooden letter-box outside. They would appear overnight in a black march up or down a wall, tens of thousands of them in a malign streak that one shaved away with a knife into a dustpan. One anointed the bare wall-trail with kerosene but they'd be back, maybe behind my books, where they did a lot of damage. A horizontal column of what to me were ordinary ants plodded right round the large room on the wall about a foot off the ground for a few days each summer. It seemed to be their idea of a holiday as they left things as they were and disappeared. The odd mouse or rat had to be seen to and I made a vow never again to live on the ground floor in India. A cockroach would flit alarmingly across the bathroom at times but the species usually crept or lay and one would scuttle an individual back into the drain it had emerged from. A Bengali cockroach is an *arshola*, felicitously enough, a large, repellent but fairly innocuous being. What else? Gecko lizards on the walls, that paid their rent by keeping down the *arshola* race and others. There were more of them in my next flat, that was on the fourth floor, where they came in through ventilator openings and provided a rather wearisome form of kinetic art with their amazing suction-pad feet across wall and ceiling. One should warm up the Tate Modern and festoon the walls with them. Once I watched a *tik-tiki* (gecko) hypnotise a large moth. A stalking gecko is a wonder to behold: it will freeze, after an eternity move fractionally forward, with infinite patience await the instant and dart and strike. In this case as it got close it appeared to fix the moth with its eyes; the victim made no move as the eyes crouched before it for an appreciable time before the coup. I thought a paragraph would do to sum up the unasked-for living partners of my stay but memories swarm and buzz: I will not be able to stop their further incursion into the account here and there. But less copiously henceforth.

I was in the Park Street flat for nearly four years and by the time I moved on was at home in the city. I wrote a lot of poetry and found a voice, as they say, as a lyrical translator of the most famous volume of Rabindranath's Tagore's poems. 'Gitanjali' has an exceptional history. The title means 'Song Offerings' and they are devotional pieces of freshness and beauty: 157 short poems each with a metaphysical point and a flow that fits finely into song. And that is exactly what happened: Rabindranath turned 91 of them into songs either as he wrote them as poems or shortly afterwards. The song-text is often abbreviated and employs refrain to a greater extent; and the sung pace is slower than that of the spoken poem. As songs they are infinitely popular. The minority that remain solely as poems are less known; and the words of the others are met in melody, for the most part; so that the identity of the original volume of verse is compromised. But I was fascinated by the sequence both in its variety and as a single long poem, and re-created it in English without regard to the songs so many had become. For it is inspired poetry.

The original volume was further obscured by Rabindranath's own rendering of about a third of them into English poetic prose. He published these in England in 1912, mixing in about fifty versions of his poems from other volumes, to create an entirely new sequence – and won the Nobel Prize as a result! This was awarded in 1913, the English book keeping the Bengali title of the main contributor volume, 'Gitanjali'. The Nobel committee also saw another volume of his self-translation in similar vein, and a volume of essays written straight into English (*Sadhana* or *The Realisation of Life*), both published in 1913 – but the English 'Gitanjali' was the rage. Since then translations of 'Gitanjali' have tended to be from his English, including into other Indian languages, and there is little sense of what the originals were like or even what they were, outside Bengali-speaking areas (within them too to an extent). It is a schizophrenic literary phenomenon with all the 'Gitanjali' material – Bengali poems, Bengali songs and English prose-poems – of the very highest quality. I was content gradually to make the acquaintance of the first text and the persona within it, and to catch something of the author's artistry and love.

So I passed my days, wandering round Calcutta, seeing people, word-wrestling, teaching a little, learning to live. I had difficult moments in the flat with electricity and plumbing problems and misunderstandings with workmen, but the problems always resolved themselves; though there was a strange telephonic glitch. At different times two or three very odd people persisted in ringing me up at all hours. They didn't know me but somehow had lit on the number and revelled in the harassment. I had the impression of a touch of psychic disturbance in the urban air; but it was probably over-reaction on my part. My own psyche, tugged at by opposites, at times felt under a challenge; but always I gave myself time. Sometimes walking in this or that blighted area I experienced everything on two levels. This splendid city, this wasteland. Constant behind it lay the sense of a spirit, a female presence, a goddess, a waif. Bengal worships the female deity perhaps as much as anywhere now; and I think after experiencing their festivals my mind carried the faintest of imprints of Durga and Kali and Saraswati. But it wasn't only that. In with the violence, the choking corruption, the plague that at times seemed to haunt the city, was something I hadn't learned before to think about, that I could not help but characterise as living and female though I knew that was only a shorthand. There is a blind human situation, and an element that can seem to accompany it, that may or may not be mirage but sticks deep. The knife that scraped the *ui poka* off the wall and the pen that took on a Tagore poem did not belong to me. And on a wider level in the roads of the city I might find myself attuned to something that was or wasn't there, and back at home, in a verse of my own, address it.

*I*s it not strange, lady, that I should see
a glass metropolis? and richness carousing
over a highway of light? when I should see
a city of broken buses and brutal housing,
a slush-tide shoring up a human filth-structure,
Calcutta? Lady of cities if I should see
at times a pure and loving architecture –
is it that, near you, to your fit needs I should see?
Sometimes a grandeur sings to me. Then all
my wearied minutes pass. There is a making,
trust and strength are a city, its proud words call,
a poem outside me is built. There is a making.
A palace rises from a small poem's form ...
and you the queen, in your least woman-form.

14

In autumn for a space the city roars. This is Durga Puja, when for ten days the sense of an overpowering presence, that from day one captures the air, takes charge of existence. As the goddess Durga leaves her mountain home to revisit that of her childhood, *mahalaya* is celebrated, 'the great house'. For the first six days she is on her way. Preparations to receive her have taken over. The city becomes a household driven to honour her arrival, to welcome her, by putting on a tremendous show. But it is more than that. Insofar as it is the home of a community it is renewed at such a time; and this is the whole city and also every part of it; and every village and each part of it too. Public areas and private homes celebrate her coming and honour her going. An oceanic wave comes closer and closer, descends for four days, withdraws: and ordinary life begins again.

Work has already begun on the *pandals*, temples of bamboo and cloth to house images of Durga and her family. These temporary structures generate enormous interest: for in their outward appearance they may imitate buildings nationally or internationally well-known; while inside the images are born of a more personal aesthetic, and a deeply splendid one. They are made of clay and bamboo and straw, with an impulsive variation within a given pattern, as is the Indian way; and they tell (or remind of) an epic element in the living story. Five figures on a great screen, Durga in the centre and her four children, present a family front that in a loving and practical way attends to almost everything. Thrift, song, military tactics, business enterprise, and a multitude of related areas, are looked after by the two daughters and the two sons, divinities all; while at the centre Durga slays the demon that was about to topple the universe. Animals and birds are there too, the vehicles of the divine, and a buffalo as the demon's alter ego. Shiva, Durga's husband and one of the great triumvirate of Indian deities, is unobtrusively present. The screen (the *chalchitra*) offers this magnificent array in *pandal* after *pandal*, each one different, some richer in colour than others, some in trappings of grandeur, some in an everyday simplicity, some in comic touches, some in a fierce intensity, some in a flowing grace. All communicate the pure fact of the story both lingeringly, as one starts to take in the individual craftsmanship, and at once, in the ray of a stab-instant.

An area in North Calcutta where the images are traditionally made is awe-inspiring to visit in the months before the festival. In dark small workshops half-formed figures of lion (Durga's vehicle) or swan (Saraswati's), buffalo, snake (in league with the demon), and of the divinities themselves smile serenely or claw apart the heavens. Durga's children are Saraswati and Lakshmi and

Ganesh and Kartik, all known to the whole of India, and Ganesh more than all, with his elephant trunk and plump belly imparting a marvellous confidence to any enterprise. Durga has ten arms and (finally) a weapon in each hand. Yet she is kindly; and more, she is not only the mother but the daughter too, and the small girl. But more than all a wedded woman on an annual trip to her father's house with her children, her husband staying behind (hence Shiva's muted appearance). She is every Indian bride who has left home to marry and takes the children back on a visit to the family – that by a sleight of imaginative thought and deed is now any and every group of people that has put up a *pandal* and arranged for the images to be installed. There is a stream of shifting identity in Hinduism that distinguishes it from the prosaic absolutism of some other religions. To see it all on its way in the craftsmen's sheds in Kumartuli is phenomenal.

The craftsmen have a tradition: a handful of earth is taken from outside a prostitute's home to initiate the moulding of the first image. No-one is left out from the festival of womanhood.

On the seventh day Durga arrives and the images are alive. Momentous events take place on this and the next three days. But the first six, that are lived at once in a thrill of impending carnival, and in a deeper and more passionate sense of anticipation, have their own helter-skelter momentum. On the morning of *mahalaya* hundreds of thousands listen to a long musical programme broadcast in the small hours of songs of welcome (*agaman*) and Sanskrit verse. Later that day men come to the river to remember their dead fathers and forefathers. Priests (some mere boys) will chant mantras and purify offerings made to the river and to the dead. After these solemnities the community hums for a time: everyone buys new clothes, fairgrounds are set up, strung with fantastic multi-coloured lights, Durga appears on billboards advertising as it may be shoes, everything is transformed to make-believe, and everyone feels real. So it proceeds to *bodhan*, the rite on the seventh day when the images take on life and a great drama is played out as new.

I had found a goddess. R. was younger than me and there were greater differences. But whenever I thought about them they vanished. People and poetry were her core. One evening in the Park Street flat I knew she was anxious to get away for a family reason but we had some people round and she stayed to see they were well looked after. What I couldn't understand was that she wouldn't interrupt a conversation between some of them to say the food was ready. She stopped me from doing so and it went on for some time. Finally they broke up and she brought on the food; and in due course made her exit. I realised a sensitivity in her beyond that which I was inured to. A conversation is to be respected.

But she was no shy violet and when we clashed it was audible. There was a well of uncertainty in each of us as to the need or possibility of commitment. I had come to a new continent ready for anything but that; in a sense I had travelled five thousand miles away from it. There had been the occasional short-lived affair in England and (shorter) in India since lighting out on my own. My first marriage had been unexpected, spontaneous, a success in some ways; nevertheless (in the nature of an early marriage) it had loomed up like something on a conveyor belt. That was not the case now. On my side misgivings met in an unholy alliance with stronger doubts on hers. Yet we were together, if still living apart, each sounding out a blind and, for her at times, a painful way. Division ran through us and in a strange way made us one.

Near the end of Durga Puja is a moment at once of playfulness and of a piercing sadness. Durga's visit is coming to a close and she is to return with her brood to her husband Shiva in their Himalayan home. What in prosaic fact will happen is that her image along with all the others will be launched into the Hooghly, the local stretch of the Ganga (River Ganges), to break up and disappear. But she is on her way back home. Married women (who know the pain of leaving the childhood home to marry, and at the end of a visit thereafter) circle the *chalchitra*, apply *sindoor* (the red sign of a married woman) to the crown of Durga's head, and to one another. Some silently weep. R. had left home long since and the situation was untypical in other respects, but looking back I seem to recognise an aspect of her pain, and of mine also.

*N*o you don't see. You hear my words.
You hear my silence. You know who I am.
I am a foreigner. In your eye
I am a foreign body. How can you see?
I see less. I hear your silence
and not many words. In my hearing
language is dislodged. I will learn your words.
Still too few. Can I know who you are?
What does silence say? It is where distance
is person not country. It is where language
is song not speech. It is where you and I
allow a third to be. I love the silence
that knocks at a door. I love the silence
that offers welcome. That is a new being.

15

The chance hand of chaos has a part in the action of an Indian festival. In the first week of Durga Puja, as the goddess makes her way towards her ancestral home, West Bengal simmers in a blind unrest. Other states, more concerned with other divinities, at their times of annual *puja* (worship and honour) are as apt to be visited by a touch of frenzy. On my earlier, exploratory trip to the country I went to the city of Puri in Orissa for *rath yatra*, the tugging of three gigantic chariots four kilometres from the centre of town to the sea.

I have never seen anything like it. The chariots, elaborate open trucks, each transport a divine personage and about fifty men and youths wildly festooned on platforms up and down the massive height of the statue. Ropes trail from the chariots and more men and youths rush into the road to grasp them and assist the sacred journey. The road is crazily packed with onlookers, as are the roofs nearby including temple-tops, one of which broke when I was there with three deaths resulting (I did not see it). I was mesmerised by the unconscionably slow passage of the vehicles. As they made their way priests blessed the sandy road before them and people dashed up and buried their heads in the wheel-tracks behind them. I understood for the first time that the epic scale of things has its own effect and is valid. But a war was going on in my head. The danger to the onlookers was considerable as anybody could simply rush in and try to seize a rope, and did so; the crowd rippled with the smallest and weakest in terror; why couldn't they rope off corridors, I thought, and have pre-selected rope-pullers to do the thing safely and sensibly? And as I thought it I cursed the Westerner in myself. Jagannatha, the principal deity, an avatar of Lord Vishnu, was in touch with his people, and by these means he was alive.

I had read and forgotten the narrative, what was happening, the mythic rationale. All I saw was the colossal deliberateness of the gods taking the air. It was a violently hot day, my head ached, I gave up on the spectacle and the internal discussion and went to the sea myself. The current was too strong for swimming but I waded and cooled down; and ended up in the hotel arguing with a Dutchman about foreign aid. It is eighteen years ago as I write and still I see the vast contraptions roll past me, packed with humanity, occupied by the divine, and simply watch.

Back to Durga Puja, where I knew, and felt, much more of the underlying story. Yet still one is primarily a witness. One sees in the first days the *pandals* going up and a furious interest in the various designs, with various businesses offering awards, both for the outward look and the momentary immortal screens within. Prizes are announced at the end of the festival. Art and architecture students earn a handy bonus contributing advice and expertise. Everyone's shopping, mainly for new clothes to present to other members of the family. One is dressed new in the great days. Every area is involved: Mohammed Ali Park is always vying for top honours for its *pandal* and *chalchitra*. A Muslim neighbourhood can star in a Hindu festival. Later I'll comment on the great days, the seventh to the tenth; but this is the build-up; and a buzz runs up and down the city's spine. And there is a sense of being carried along, helpless, a speck of dust, surrendered to the sweep and spin of a puff of wind, there in a kind of erratic drift. I am focussing on an aspect one tends to let be and take for granted; for the random is everywhere and in everything (as physics reveals), and it goes a little way to understanding a part of what was happening.

It is not only the times of intense community awareness that I seem to know more of, if I look at this side of things, but also more personal matters. The precariousness of the situation between R. and myself was part of a hidden festival, an unannounced visitation, a different surrender. Without any particular wish on my part to understand more on either the public or the private side, something seems to declare itself, and it is to do with the open admission of the awry current into the mainstream. It is little enough; it needs to be said; and once said it lets me alone, easier in myself, able again to look at other matters.

I was invited to teach on Sundays in Khelaghar, a school for orphans in an outlying area of the city. The name means 'House of Play' and it was started by a lady who had been close to Tagore. She was now dead and the present headmistress was an invalid but able to meet the challenge and more than that, to redefine it. I knew immediately it would be a privilege to work for her as a teacher. She was a very remarkable person, now also gone. The school had a Tagorean character in its closeness to Nature and its sense of the individual. I got to know a boy and a girl, both about fifteen and both in their different ways charged with a powerful, charismatic, innocent intent. I wanted to take them under my wing: they were both very bright, they wanted to do well, they needed an anchor. I stopped myself however; and fairly soon the weekly lessons came to an end. I heard that later they had each run up against the school to some extent. I think something in them needed more room; I would have liked to help, but let the chance go. Sometimes a Westerner unofficially adopts a child in need almost on an impulse – and sometimes officially, returning to his or her country with a cherished object. I did not feel it was what I had come to Calcutta to do and kept a distance. But there was a recognition between the three of us of something in common; and I think – as well as a love of words and a touch of the maverick in each of us – it was a sense of being at sea, of letting the waves wash one up against whatever shores (or rocks) they would, with an inner confidence as to the outcome. It was of course entirely unspoken: they were courteous, as all Indian children are at school; and no doubt were unable to think of me as on the same level as them in any way. Still, I felt there was a recognition.

As a teacher one lives a life of brief friendships. One has known many thousands of children, almost all of whom will remember one, and almost all of whom one has forgotten.

Still there is a part of one's mind that is populated by interesting characters, independent souls, minds of great promise, emergent personalities, overcharged psyches. For some reason these two at Khelaghar are with me. I suppose one stays friends with people who are no longer there. And in this case, with people whose lives had been hit – as mine was early on – by a dislodging force; and who dealt with existence in its waywardness. God knows what they are up to now. I taught them in an amazing classroom: it should be repeated round the world.

*F*irst up some steps: and then a room without walls.
   Supports for the roof – and in between, some trees.
What is this room in which the fresh air falls?
A place in which to work and be at ease.
It is the loveliest classroom. To one who has been
clamped between walls of learning; who in turn
has caged young minds in crowded Nature-mean
high-rise low-vision London schools – to learn
and teach here, is a breath of what may be.
And yet perhaps I took away the walls
for one or two, at times, when I was able.
Part of all making is a making-free.
This tree-room lies inside the world's school-halls:
a boy and girl, a teacher, and a table.

16

The goddess Durga visibly trounces the malign. The magnificent demon at the base centre of the screen is overpowered. Invisibly too she is triumphant, her power casts a wider spell, we are reassured as to something beyond the reliability of a defence system. She has taken on evil and more; a lacuna in what we know of being is no more; in her presence we are untroubled by what may now be called existentialist pressures that have always nudged out a space for themselves. One reason for divinity is to supervene upon the uncertain, to close the circle on the random. The sense of completeness as a person that one can feel I am sure at any age back to early childhood, in the full nearness, so to speak, to the divine, is to do with the removal of an obstacle in this space too.

It is of course an illusion. But it has a bearing on the real. What we perceive as true greatness is to an extent founded upon life-achievement that has met this demon, unmalign but at some level more terrifying than the other, and gained the advantage. Whether or not we shall always use the example of a divine figure or figures to point the way, some sort of journey to inner riches will no doubt continue to torment us forward. Whatever we call the obstacle, the inner shifts and uncertainties of knowing and being, to give it an anodyne phrase, there are those who take its measure. They are of flesh and blood like us, and a few go on to do superlative things, to work wonders, and shape civilisations.

I make no apology for returning to Tagore. When *Time Magazine* was looking for its Person of the Millennium and inviting suggestions I sent in a lengthy entry detailing his contribution, as I saw it: no reply. Opening a few doors in his poetic mansion to make a handful of imperfect casts, to put the translator's job unpoetically enough, had brought me into contact with his thought and art; and merely living in Calcutta, too, made me close somehow. I also spent a great deal of time for a year in a village outside the city where his lingering presence is all but a palpable fact. In Santiniketan and nearby the poet gave himself to certain endeavours in the fields of education and rural development that continue, and keep up a sense of him, a century later. It is the complete persona that I would dearly like to convey a sense of, though I may not be able to. My apprehension of it over the years I think helped me to deal with the wayward and erratic in what I felt around me and within myself. It was simply like a friend in the distant background.

His works and days were multifarious and fine, both on the artistic level in a number of media and as a leader, teacher and public speaker, nationally and internationally known. But whatever shortlist one makes of his achievements one omits items that clamour for a place. Eventually one has to echo George Bernard Shaw's "Stupendranath Begorr!" and settle for the incomplete. Behind his poetry, songs, paintings, novels and short stories, essays and text-books and studies on this or that topic, his dance dramas and plays, and the school and the university he founded and worked for unremittingly (both at Santiniketan); and behind the rural projects, and the international lecture tours; and behind his driven commitment to fostering a mature sense of social and political identity at home and abroad, and so much more, was a gentle soul. In all sorts of details he affected Bengali culture, from instituting new festivals to the use of a less formal written language to the encouragement of folk art. He is in the air: but I see something more personal is needed, and though it may give offence to some I shall relate a love story that in its lightest outline tells the man.

Kadambari was the girl-bride of a much older brother of his, Jyotirindranath. He was a musician and artist of considerable repute and took a great interest in the boy as he grew up. Kadambari was about two years older than Rabindranath and all through their teens they were close. In a Bengali household a younger brother-in-law is sometimes afforded a position of especial tenderness; and without doubt for a short time the two young adults shared an intimacy of the mind and heart that Rabindranath treasured all his days. A marriage was arranged for him rather hastily; she helped (following tradition) to find the bride; soon after the wedding she killed herself. Rabindranath's deep love for her became the inspiration of his poetry. He was never explicit: a departed lover reappears at moments in several poems and one or two notable passages of prose; here and there he acknowledges his debt to her as the wellspring of his poetic life; not once does he name her.

When I think of what the Western media would have made of this, had Tagore been one of their own, and compare it with the sensitiveness of his countrymen on the issue, I am glad for his sake he was not born here. It has not been explored, very little speculated on: it is as if the characters are respected as living people. (Not that that means much in the West.) Whether or not they slept together is of no concern. Whether Kadambari is the mysterious lady who reappears in his work, indescribably close and dear, I think is: and after all this time I think it can be said that it is so. There is no proof, but any number of pointers; and over the rest of his life it is as if in a private meeting now and then he remained in touch with her, staying within the bounds of decorum; but not forgetting her, and what he had been to her and she to him.

His own wife died after nineteen years of an affectionate marriage. He did not re-marry. Two of his five children died soon after, in 1903 and 1907, each aged a little over ten years old. Another daughter was to die later in her early thirties. His mother had passed away when he was thirteen. He lived on, unafraid of death, but more, as if privileged by the union to come, while living a life as far removed from a "death-wish" as is to be imagined. He lived fully, a quite magnificent writer, in my view second to none as a being on Earth. He was a spiritual leader for the time, with no "hotline" to God; he understood the journey of the individual both as its own small cosmic instance and as an event in the modern world; his was an existence resonant with the human way. He made mistakes, had his limitations; but he lives in the minds and hearts of his countrymen and women; and it is not inconceivable that one day, his work or the essence of it translated into this language and that, a small ripple may begin its way over the globe of a visionary good sense and an understanding to the depths.

Amongst Bengali intellectuals there has been something of a reaction against Tagore, that is natural enough. For one thing, he is no modernist. He understood modernism, as is shown by the phantasmagoric suddenness and stillness of his paintings; but did not need to turn his words that way. There is still a difficulty in coming to terms with the extent of the Tagorean phenomenon. Scholars are impatient with the uncritical acclaim that he still receives, and I shall be accused of it no doubt. But after all the grand words it is simply as a person that he makes an impression on my hard-headed old soul, unexpectedly offering a direction.

*M*y poet, you have made me weep.
    At the sad point the mind swings on
in life's space-hazard ... you have seen
what shines, what will shine, what has shone.
My elder brother, you have held
my arm and told me of the way.
Flickeringly the late sky's gold
foretells love in my later day.
But to be lost! but to be lost!
From the safe tethering-rope to part
of vanities, till love's arrest ...
what dream is it, friend of my heart,
you whisper of? And yet tears spring
for love's song, that I too will sing.

17

Gradually in the account itself it is my hope that the festival of Durga Puja will act, in touches here and there, as a kind of fermenting agent. The great days from the seventh to the tenth (literally so in the Bengali) have yet to be encountered; the whole teems insensibly in the background of living in West Bengal. To know it is to happen is a part of being there. But there is a secular festival, as I like to think of it, of scarcely less significance to the life of the capital, to which it is specific: the Calcutta Book Fair.

For the last day or two in January and the first ten or eleven in February a part of the Maidan, a long green strip at the city centre, is a riot of many colours. About a thousand stalls, attractively designed and painted plasterboard one-room shops, with a counter and chairs and a display of books inside, are at once there, an expressive miniature metropolis risen from nowhere, with a myriad small avenues and some larger, more open squares. Each stall, named by the owner in Bengali or English script and allotted a number by the Book Fair committee, seems to take part in a festival of the word, a thriving unit. Though some are less visited than others each is a centre of its own, of conversation as well as commercial transaction. One is there for the books of course yet not that alone. Massive crowds swirl around the Fair every afternoon till after dark, the grass is trampled away (fortunately it is the dry season), individuals often meet for the first time in a year, two old men argue in the middle of a path, a young girl sells xeroxed copies of her short stories at a rupee a page, an artists' enclave (Montmartre) has paintings and live sketching, long tables in an open section display magazines of prose and poetry from all over the state (a famous section this, Little Magazines), a recitation or a song sounds over the mikes, outside a restaurant tent one sips tea and wonders why Calcutta is the only place where this happens. All other book fairs are trade fairs but this is for the general public. The entrance fee is no more than a bus fare. As well as the posh bookshops that have their own smart and spacious stalls, and well-known publishers that may have a splendid marquee, there are any number of humbler ventures. People will save up to have a book of their poems privately published and sell it at a bookshop's stall. There is an international flavour with a pavilion of books from Bangladesh, and France, and so on; and each year the Fair takes a certain country as a theme (in 2006 it was Spain). People visit from far and wide in the state. It is opened and closed with a touch of fanfare and ceremony, exists for its twelve days as a colossal hubbub at the city's heart, and disappears as if it had never been.

The first time I went there was a bewilderingly long queue at the Fair's central square doubling back and back on itself, many hundreds of people who stood without moving on for hours. I asked what everyone was waiting for. For the West Bengal Government official stall to open. It had published a subsidised edition of the writings of Tagore in fifteen volumes. How far from the West I felt. It was, and is, a humbling moment.

Books are sold in the Fair at a discount and everywhere people are rustling over them, text-books, religious books, children's books, or the various selections of an emporium such as Oxford Book Store of Park Street in its smart tent. Hundreds of thousands of ordinary people will make a purchase or two over the duration and spend hours looking at books, considering them, discussing them, close to them. It is no accident that the Fair overlaps with the special day of the goddess of learning, Saraswati. The whole occasion seems in her honour somehow (though she is entirely in the background: no explicit link is made at all). While there are stalls with what might be called cheap reading-matter, thrillers and comics and the like, it's a surprisingly small percentage. (Similarly there are no smutty newspapers in the state.) In a way it's a not unserious occasion.

And it's one of a casual delight. A touch of carnival atmosphere comes out as the evening darkens: balloon-sellers, maybe someone on stilts, as the crowd begins to drift, as slowly as hens beginning to meander in the general direction of the coop at dusk, towards the gates. There's a famous fish shop (Bengal is crazy about fish) that has an ardent following: a snack at BenFish makes the day. And the whole afternoon has been one of ease in high definition, so to speak, the city in small, a freedom in the open. Ice-creams, soft drinks (alcohol on the premises is inconceivable), teenagers at their cell-phones, students lolling here and there, and a commonwealth of world-citizens going about their business. It is wholly secular; but this is the clue about Indian gods and goddesses, that they can be as well. Which is why, when I think of the Book Fair for any length of time, somewhere Saraswati stands in the shadows, invisible in the background.

I had my own stall one year, or rather a third of a stall. One of my partners in the enterprise ran a small concern called Avant-Garde Press, which appeared in Bengali (transliterated) on the shop front, next to a legend that advertised my poems and from which I derived a childish pleasure. I had a number of Writers Workshop volumes out by that time and too many copies of each, and some poetry pamphlets with Avant-Garde also, and thought I'd try to sell a few. I did, a very few, and spent a lot of time at the stall with no customers quite enjoying being a part of it all. Then one afternoon sheer horror struck the Fair.

I had left the stall in the charge of a couple of students who assisted Avant-Garde and the third party, to wander here and there; and came out into one of the large squares where a sizeable crowd stood stock-still watching a thin trail of smoke rise from the top of a kitchen-tent. As I too watched, the tent burst into flame and at once two or three others nearby did the same. Suddenly everyone was running everywhere. I scooted back to my stall and asked the students to start taking the books out to a spot in the open (fortunately we were on the perimeter). One of them stayed with the books while I finished off the carrying with the other, who started to panic, trying to dismantle the empty stall. By now the fire was unstoppable. All the stalls in the main area were ablaze. The flames were sky-monsters. I managed to dissuade the young man left with me from taking the stall down – it was too bulky to take away in any case – and for an hour or more waited by the stall watching the fantastic sheets of fire in the sky to see if they would dip our way. Our area of the ground, with a bare stretch between it and the rest, was the only part untouched by the flames, and it was crammed with people who had fled the other parts but didn't want to leave the site. I thought there might be a stampede if the flames licked our way and kept an eye on the possible exits. It was the only fire of its kind I've been anywhere near and I was stunned by the shattering might of the roaring sails and how helpless we were against them. At last it was clear they were no threat and we collected the books and restored them to the shelves.

The single human casualty, I heard later, was a man who had suffered a heart attack scrabbling through the ashes for his books. We were in the five per cent or so of the Fair that had been untouched. The site was closed down for a few days but re-opened before the end of the allotted time. Now and then I am there in mind, outside the stall as if I had not moved, half-looking up at the leaping sails.

*F*ather your hand raised terrible in the sky
    dwarfs our book-parades, our babble of print,
as all the living blood of words springs high.
Father the vanity of recorded signs
you crush to ashes. How puny we are
I think in the minutes before the stampede. It is all
                                    down to, up to

the wind. And all I can think of
as I see a fantasy of book-stalls burning to the heavens
is wind-direction and where the main gate is. Father
I saw no stampede. And my books were lucky,
returned to an intact stall. But in your thunderous
flame behind the line of events, enfold me,
take my words take my books take my vanities Lord.
O blaze your poetry as you darken mine.

18

Later that evening, exhausted in my flat, I rang a lady to say that I wouldn't be able to go to see her daughter dance. The family had invited me; the dancer was just starting her career; her mother refused to accept my absenting myself. It seemed I was to inform Europe of the young talent. I said repeatedly that I knew nothing of dance or dancers or dance critics; it didn't matter. I said there'd been a fire at the Book Fair and I'd had to look after my stall and was very tired. She knew of the fire but it didn't matter. Finally with an apology I put the phone down on the still polite but imperiously demanding voice. What was a fire, after all, to the international reputation of her daughter?

I was reminded of a passage from a Tagore poem. Malati is a Calcuttan girl who falls in love. The young man who has stolen her heart – 'let's call him Naresh' – goes to England to further his studies and writes to her of his new friend, Lizzie, in terms that leave Malati in no doubt that the game is up. She plots an imaginary revenge. Saratchandra Chatterjee, a very popular writer, will write a short story in which a character called Naresh will repeatedly fail his examinations, while a Malati will triumph in Mathematics at Calcutta University and be invited to Europe, where she will be hailed 'not only as a learned woman, but as a woman. / Let the world-captivating spell of her / work its power – not in a witless land, / but where there are discerning minds, great hearts – / the English, the Germans, the French.' A dazzling reception in her honour, with Naresh cowering in the background 'with his bevy of oh-so-extraordinary girls', sees her in paradise: 'Imagine, there is a perfect storm of flattering words, / in the midst of which she is walking casually, / like a sailing-boat over waves. / They see her eyes and all are whispering – / they say, India's moist clouds and burning sunlight / have met in that bewitching glance. / (Here I will say in private, / the Creator did indeed bestow a special favour on my eyes – / I have to say this for myself, / for to date it has not been my fortune to meet / a European to appreciate them.)' And she is returned to who she is and where she is, with an exquisite pathos bearing out the poem's title, 'Ordinary Girl'. As she says earlier to Saratchandra, 'Name your heroine Malati. / That's my name. / There's no fear of its being found out, / there are any number of Malatis in Bengal, / and all are ordinary girls – / they don't know French or German, / they know how to cry.'

Tagore knew what he was about. He wrote the poem some sixty-five years before my 'phone conversation but he could have had it in mind. Incidentally I came upon a delicacy of feeling with regard to this poem that made me think twice about my own reaction to it. I said to someone that I enjoyed Tagore's touches of humour in it. "No, no, it's not a funny poem." He was shocked I should think so. I said that of course the portrait of a hurt girl wasn't a comic one; but there was an enjoyable satiric touch in one or two places. Still the shock. I was allowed to say the author had a twinkle in his eye at these moments, but untwinklingly allowed; a sense lingered of my misunderstanding or disrespect as to what mattered. Interested as to the very slight and yet real offence my comment had occasioned I discussed the poem with a number of people at different times and invariably seemed to touch the same nerve. I expect the author himself would not have been entirely happy to hear my comment: for (I concluded) the coarse grain in the mix that is humour in the West can be discomforting to the Bengali sensibility. One cannot leave the main matter in abeyance, if it is to do with a person's feelings; to take such things for granted may be to forget them; and in the West there is a whole realm of the precious and intimate that we have cast aside. Our standing next to the offerings of Nature, to the hours of the day and night, is far less of a privilege to us than to an Indian, who is likely to know medicinal facts and mythical stories about one and have songs or tunes to hum to accompany the other. And so our standing next to the people about us is affected. On the other hand, in the detached or objective way of looking at things, that is the more needed the more complex daily life becomes, analytical accuracy proceeds at all costs. The difference of mind I came up against in conversational references to 'Ordinary Girl' was the tiniest straw in the wind, itself no doubt misinterpreted, as to what that cost may be.

Irony is more or less absent in Indian literature. It is there in everyday life, in black humour in this or that situation, though probably less so than in many cultures. There's certainly an irony as I see it in the seeking of European approval in aesthetic matters. Rather it should be the other way about.

Comparative exercises can mean little. R. and I went to Digha, the nearest sea resort to Calcutta. One morning we waded and I swam a little, in a splashing throng of a hundred or two; the women and girls in sari or *salwar kameez* or frock, the men and boys in shorts; there was nothing but the water and light of holiday, nothing could be more carefree. An hour later we were drinking coffee outside a small restaurant at the top of some steps overlooking the bathing area. Everything was as before. Then a youth was shouting and running by the water, *Phire ay, phire ay!* Come back, come back! Everyone was at once out of the water, that proceeded to shudder and boil and froth as if in some monstrous grip. We had come down the steps at the commotion and the waves slapped across the terrace where we'd been sitting at peace. The boy's brother had been swimming on the outskirts of the group and gone under; no-one had noticed at the time. Now it was impossible to go back in. It was as if the sea mocked whoever might dare to. He was lost. R. and I left the area and went for a long walk that took up most of the day.

We moved slowly along a pristine area of the beach, picking up shells, examining tiny intricate tracks of sand-insects, and inland for a little, through a couple of villages, round to we were staying. When it was dark we revisited the shore, not where we had been swimming, and saw a silent group of people. We approached and saw the corpse of the youth who had drowned that morning. They had found it a few moments before, washed up there; the legs and arms were curled up a little and the body looked strangely small. For a long time we stood there. I wish I could paint the thoughts of the sea that came to me: I certainly couldn't put it in words. My thoughts, not the sea's, yet ...

Or it could be a symphony that no musician could compose. The colours of the large shells, that we had picked up and put back at noon, and the green of the village fields, and our love, and the knowledge that everything has an end, and the distant restless din from which so much has come. Wilfred Owen has said something of it in his poem 'Futility'; but it was not futility I felt in that presence, but the sadness and the beauty of life.

*T*here was a beach, cleaned by the sea, which was
    for us a new face of the world. We saw
miraculous shells; and god-like tracery
in sand of tiniest creatures. It was like
a welcoming-day, admission to a hall
of being.

   In the dark we came back there
and discovered a knot of people, silent.
A young man had been lost from that same beach
that morning, swimming: here was his dead body.
In sudden grief you turned to my live arms.
Dear, we are the patterns in the sand
I thought, and those brave colourful shells
we make, life makes ... *I listened to the sea.*
You could not have been closer or more far.

19

When I moved to the Park Street flat my new landlord gave me some advice: "Keep out of politics." I had no intention of tapping on any doors that led into the performing dogs' circus that is always something of a witless diversion; and where I was, as the papers reminded one every day, a dangerous one. The dogs bit. Killings related to political activism were commonplace. At election time there was a curious double effect of health and chronic disease: on the one hand democracy showed it was alive and well, after a fashion; while on the other the nastiest human streak there is crept to the surface, the self-righteously vicious. It is easy to be very cynical about voting under threat, as so many do, especially in the villages; and there were times I saw it all as the merest fraud – "democracy" a great white tablecloth draped over the land for show, to be scooped up and twisted relentlessly by local barons, no more than the latest device in the rule by fear. But India has proved herself as a democracy nonetheless, notably in 2004 when the ruling BJP Party was unexpectedly kicked out and its slogan 'India Shining' given its notice as only the people can deliver it, land-wide. So I didn't tap on any doors but still listened to the din; and of course much was done by good people that was admirable, to offer a tantalising glimpse of an upturn in the fortunes of the land. But it is never that easy. It will take a century or two yet for 'democracy' to settle down in India, and in the meantime anything may happen, the borders may change; and yet, more surely than with any country on Earth, one would suppose the centre to hold. To a Westerner it's a different political noise, more urgent and rasping than the rallying or reproachful tone back home. From a distance then, and making little out, one listened.

A couple of election anecdotes. A decent, educated young man votes about twenty times. The (ruling) Communist party has given him a list of names on various electoral rolls that are unlikely to turn up: they are away, ill or dead. He impersonates them. Each time he votes a finger is inked but he has also been issued with a chemical solution to get rid of it. He is sincere in believing it is his duty to do all he can for his party. And a boy who can be no more than twelve is photographed voting and interviewed by a journalist. His picture appeared in an English-language medium paper with a promise: "If the Communists don't win I'm going to bomb the *thana*." (The *thana*, with a soft aspirated *t*, is the police station, a word everyone uses. The interview would have been in Bengali, maybe Hindi.) The casual acceptance of acts and statements such as these, that are not at all unusual, is a slight shock the first time round to the visitor and then of course hardly noticed: it is the way things are.

The Communist Party by no means has a monopoly on such expedients though in the size and scale of its lawlessness it vastly outstrips its main rivals in the state, when it comes to vote-getting. The above examples pale into insignificance. It has never been the party of national government, though it has contributed to a central ruling coalition; but it has been of great historical importance in India, and at the time of writing as the Communist Party of India (Marxist) leads three state governments: West Bengal, Kerala and Tripura. In West Bengal it has been the ruling party continuously for over thirty years. It made its mark in the late 'seventies with some valuable measures to do with local government and the re-allocation of surplus land; and since then has achieved comparatively little, beyond tightening its hold on power. And yet symbolically it means a great deal. In its very existence the Communist ideal is not forgotten, though in practice the party is mindful of the advantages of capitalism. The unspoken struggle for the soul of the nation is almost unbearable to contemplate, with the North American example exerting a massive pull in the direction of an accumulation of commodities, and the presence of the gods of the land, besides which the nine generations of the USA are a puff of wind, silently clamouring for India's insight and knowledge to be remembered. The Left Front, a collective left-wing party bloc, and the Bharatiya Janata Party (BJP), that has been in and out of national government, both in their different ways uphold the sense of the deeper vision, though they are often at odds. I felt honoured to be in a state with a Communist party in charge, though I hated what it did; and so the dialogue, like an imponderable turning of the soil, within each individual and over the whole land, goes on.

It is remarkable, and a little disturbing, to meet as many discerning people as I did over the years, to whom Stalin was not a gigantically flawed leader but on the contrary an icon: as if I had entered a time warp. My parents in the Second World War had revered him for a short time; and who is to say that as with Mao Zedong, despite the appalling and insane direction the policies took, and the terrifying momentum they gathered, there is not a seed of human thought deserving of some memorial? At any rate, perverse as it may be, I was glad there was a Lenin Sarani ('Street') in Calcutta. I was stuck in a slow-moving stream in it once in a taxi, and was startled out of my reverie by a clunk as the cab knocked against the one in front. It happened again and I exclaimed at the driver, who looked all of sixteen, and was laughing fit to bust. Another tap and more hysterics; and our taxi drew level with the one in front it had been casually attacking. A boy drove that too, also helpless with laughter. "Friend," gasped my driver, "friend." I rather think Lenin, who could lose himself in games with small children and was by no means as humourless as his successor, would have enjoyed the moment.

A memorial, yes; but active continuation? Perhaps we have to keep trying. A politician of rare potential emerged recently in Calcutta and was very prominent in my time there. She is not a Communist, but (in my view) embodies the ideal behind that party, long since lost, in terms absolutely right for India. Mamata Banerjee has been in and out of the national government as a Minister but has proved unable to shake the ruling party in her home state. She is a driven force, impelled solely by a concern for the ordinary working person, and for a society freed of the dreadful corruption that has attached itself to all positions of power. Nevertheless the party she founded, Trinamool ('Grass Roots'), soon became tarred with the same brush as its opponents, countering violence with violence, despite her best efforts. She has not surrounded herself with the best of advisors and at times may have been too theatrical; yet she is still a national figure as well as someone with real influence in her own state. I harbour a hope that West Bengal will yet wake up to the treasure they have in her as a representative of all that is straight and true at the heart of the land. *

To get away from Calcutta I took a train sometimes to Darjeeling, a renowned hill station in the Himalayan foothills. One walks up and up and finally emerges onto the Mall at the top of the town, a lovely place especially in the late afternoon. I was told that during the Raj only white people were allowed there except for those serving the officers and their families with food, or providing entertainment and so forth. I don't know if this is correct but in essence it was probably so, and it sticks in the gullet even now, so far away. There are so many contradictions to take in in India; and in Darjeeling as well as the refreshing holiday atmosphere there was a constant reminder of something else, in the porters toiling up and down the hill carrying tourists' luggage. It spoke not of the Raj but of inequalities at all times, injustices everywhere.

* Mamata Banerjee became Chief Minister of West Bengal (now Paschimbanga) in 2011.

S hapes. Voices. Cool light. Images
    in ocean-mist of hills, mist-villages,
a day of Himalayan dreams,
faint bird-song, and sharp glints of streams;
and through the town a forest-fire
of stall and shop; and down from higher,
a waterfall of separate roads
past houses set on concrete rods ...
Blood. Slavery. Bent backs. Darkness
of unschooled minds pressed in earth's blackness,
of tribes that history has missed,
official blindness, power's fist.
A mountain-jewel, a blind-mist blur:
Darjeeling to a visitor.

20

I met a film-maker who told me of a documentary he'd made of a Darjeeling porter aged 100 who still went up and down the hill with tourists' luggage on his back, the traditional supporting strap straining at the forehead. The man was perfectly lucid, had no idea of who the Prime Minister might be, or of India 'out there', and looked set for a few more years. I doubted whether the century could be verified, but apparently his childhood memories bore it out. One could imagine a novel juxtaposing his comments on his work and family life and so on, and his memories, with events of 'India' and the public domain, Independence, discussions and demonstrations as to national language, national borders, national identity ... and letting the question emerge, maybe, of what a nation really is. The amalgam of public and private in what we know and see and feel is so little explored. Perhaps the documentary hinted at that; I didn't see it and don't know if it went on air or not. Calcutta is full of young film-makers following in the distant footsteps of Satyajit Ray.

He was an internationally famous film-maker who

is now a cultural icon in his home town. Any number of young Calcuttans are inspired by him. I too had my dreams, a blockbuster film epic on Tagore's life, 'Rabindranath': what a magnificent story of east and west, of the nineteenth and twentieth centuries, of love and death and song and travel, of the public and private within one existence it would be. Ray has done a minor version but the theme calls out for more. Beneath the vast and unwieldy industrial contraption of its urban sprawl, that can almost feel imposed from outside, Calcutta is very much a place of dreams.

For 140 years, from 1772, it was the capital of India. It bred and harboured great scholars, educationalists, poets and other writers, and sustains an intellectual tradition of a thrilling energy. How it works I don't know, but the collective imagination of a country can find a spot to settle, as in Athens in the fifth century B.C., and it is not done with Calcutta yet. There is nothing exclusive about it, as is evident from the burning lanterns of creativity and scholarship all over the land; but there is always a hint of intellectual renaissance in the air in Calcutta, that can send out a spark of privilege on its own account to someone living there, as at times I felt and can still feel.

There is an Indian concept of great importance that one can do with as one likes. *Maya* is all-pervading illusion, or a false sense of existence that all are subject to. It recognises that our perspective is limited in a way that (naturally) we cannot define; and it can be used with a religious intent to suggest freedom at last into a 'true' perspective; or merely left to linger in the mind, to loiter without intent there. That is where it suits me. As far as I am concerned, all that we may say or see of life may be 'wrong' and yet that living *is*, is not incorrect. And after a good deal of it, as with the porter still toiling up the hill of Darjeeling, something more can be known. We can make all the films we like, and of course that is what we do in our head in any case, with God knows what commentary, close-ups, voice-overs, music ... but the *is*, with something more, is surely what matters, and what we pass on to others. Perhaps a speck of internalised *maya*, so to speak, floats about the mind's portals in the background, as a part of any creative endeavour, whether a cinema film or the discoveries over time of a centre of learning. Or a festival.

I come to the great days of Durga Puja, *maha-saptami, maha-astami, maha-nabami. Maha* is 'great', seventh, eighth and ninth. The tenth and last, *dasami* or *bisarjan*, 'Immersion', can wait awhile. At the start of *saptami* the rite of *bodhan* takes place and the images are alive.

What happens now is more than spectacle: it *is*; and even if the whole thing's play-acting, it acts something mightily important. This *is*ness is touched upon and we have the spectacle that we never cease to have, and something more. And now I can venture upon the living stream.

On the morning of *saptami* Ganesh, the elder son of Durga, is joined in marriage to a banana-tree. This happens in Ganga, the holy river, a priest overseeing the union. Married women are alongside him in the river: their part is to worship the banana-tree branch, to bathe it, to clothe it in a sari; and they exchange *sindoor* with one another, the vermilion sign of marriage. The tree-branch is placed beside her husband in the *pandal*. Next Durga is worshipped in the form of a young girl, who will bless an old woman as she washes the little one's feet. The reversal of the norm, the younger person touching the feet of an older to receive a blessing, is moving. Durga is all womanhood including virgin child. (This rite of *kumari puja* is a relatively small affair, not carried out everywhere.) There is an offering of flowers to the goddess, *pushpanjali*; and a crescendo builds to a sacrifice. *Nabami*, the ninth day, has begun. There is an offering of fire to the goddess. 108 oil lamps burn. These days the sacrifice is usually symbolic, vegetables and fruits, such as a pumpkin, ritually halved. But especially at old rich private households a living beast is killed, though the practice is technically illegal now. I have seen young goats put to death and also a buffalo-calf. The severing of the head from the neck has to be in one clean blow or evil will befall the family. The priest-executioner knows his job. It is the moment when Durga slays the buffalo-demon who is threatening the universe. It is done. These days are one long holiday, crowds wandering from *pandal* to *pandal* to see the images and the designs, fairs going on, impromptu coffee-houses springing up and open to all hours, people in their best array, drums, song, celebration. Durga is with us. The time comes for her to depart, to return to her husband Shiva. The image-carrying screen is brought out of the *pandal*. Married women circle it, feed her *sandesh*, a traditional Bengali sweet, and offer it to one another. They put the *sindoor* mark on her head and on one another. Tears and laughter and signs of a deeper emotion are visible: there is a going, a passing, at the same time a presence beyond privilege. The final act, on the last day, is *bisarjan*, the Immersion.

The city has been awake. In a few days the reflection of the journey of each individual has passed over street and home. Great crowds go the next day to witness the leavetaking of Durga and her brood at the river. *Maya* has been embraced, and something more. A spark of life, with some of its main consequences, has been struck and is now to fade, not to die but to return.

A Westerner at the side, I think too much, *am* too little. But I too have been invited into Durga's house. Certainly something has been added to my life. After *bisarjan*, perhaps, *maya* and time are absent for a breath even as, in the familiar round, it all starts again.

*A*ll year all time, Mother, on a sharp road
I tread barefoot. I know the journey is endless,
directionless, less than a word can say.
Noise screams light blinds, Silence paralyses.
Of your grace then once a year and out of time
you come. And what is the road? It is silk that leads
to a temple. I go inside. That caterwaul
has been discarded for a song of love.
Exploding suns are your light smile. Now Mother
a self-hood loosens, as a head is freed
of a death-silence.

　　　　　Tonight the temple is empty,
on your own road the river you move so surely,
and I have walked beyond the screen of maya
with a sure step now into all year all time.

21

Every morning at the Park Street flat a packet of Mother Dairy milk was delivered to the door. On the last day of the month or the first of the next, when I paid the bill, the *dudh-wallah* (milkman) and I would have a cup of tea and each proceed to inflict a seriously-challenged form of Bengali or English on the other. But on one occasion when I opened the door he was in shock, almost tottering. I guided him to a chair. "Die – die – " he said, and to my "*ke more gecche*?" (who's died), "die – die –." He was crying. I brought tea. The monosyllable was joined by others. "Die – do – dee – die – do – dee – die –." It was surreal, all too real. As the tragic jingle went on something flickered in my mind. "Di? Dodi?" I leapt to the television and there it was, and there it stayed, day after day. My friend calmed down enough to return to his morning round.

I was shocked at the news, and in a different way and more fundamentally, at the tsunami effect it had over a vast tract of the globe. My friend's grief seemed to contain it in miniature. In Calcutta there was no change on the surface (a few shops may have shut) but the dismay could be felt, people of all backgrounds were personally affected. It was odd, but soon enough faded, with the death of Mother Teresa a few days later taking the headlines. But what was going on back home? I was only too glad to be clear of the emotional shenanigans of the U.K. If a short tremor shuddered the continents, the epicentre was off the Richter scale.

The world needs fairy-tales. But it's still disturbing to consider the attachment phenomenon as it cuts loose. The Beatles and Harry Potter are other examples. With the one, when they appeared I was a student and confidently assured my fellows of the band's inevitable disappearance in six months. I saw how wrong I was when a Scotswoman of thirty or so, a university lecturer, told me she was in love with one of them. "But what would I do with him if I had him?" Her Glasgow accent and throwaway laugh have stayed in the mind's amber these forty-five years. As for the boy wizard, who conjured for his writer a fortune from the twirls and twists of a never-ending string of cliché – I had a different accent to remember his apotheosis by. "Harry Potter, Harry Potter," croaked the book-sellers on Chowringhee, Calcutta's main street, at every Westerner who stopped at their stalls. I came to hear it as "Hari Potter", the voice of a new cult; and I am not quite sure they didn't mean it as such. A latter-day pale emulation of Lord Krishna, a deity complete with holy text – but more likely, I suppose, none was taken in by the coincidence in sound. Still if not to them, Harry is Hari, or so it would seem, to all too many.

It was with a wicked sense of relief, a month or two later

when Durga Puja was in full swing, that I saw a farewell to Diana that was almost hysterical in another way entirely. In the vicinity of the *pandal*s there are often gorgeous displays of coloured lights popping on and off, and one such told a story in three parts. First scene: the outline of a large long car. Momentary darkness. Second: the car piled up against a pillar. Momentary darkness. Third: two words, *chirabiday Diana*. Goodbye for ever Diana. Momentary darkness. The sequence repeats endlessly. I don't know about the rest of the crowd, but to me it was hilarious and moving at the same time; and after the wild and weary gale of distress that had swept the world, a touch cathartic as well.

The world needs fairy-tales. But they are watered-down now. When we had epic we didn't need the infantile Pottering-about that so many adults have taken winsomely to their heart. And it is a different brand of womanhood that lit the land with Kali.

Another form of Durga, she is Woman in her absolute power. To me she speaks for Life with all the force of Death and Night. Her *puja* comes three weeks after Durga's, a comparatively minor affair; but in the year she is immediate, timeless, present, more so perhaps than any deity. She is often portrayed with her foot on the body of her husband Shiva. In a terrible dance of triumph and anger after killing two universe-threatening demons she was herself endangering the foundations of all. Shiva lay in front of her and as she stepped on his body the horror of defiling it with her foot brought her to an awareness of what she was doing, and she was able to stop. Her tongue is extended, in recognition of the violation, it is thought.

She is worshipped at midnight before the new moon, sometimes by dacoits (violent thugs, criminals). Usually black, with a garland of skulls, she is said not to give what is expected. She is at the heart of the person who walks with death to be re-born or of the universe that has again and again been consumed in fire. R. is no believer in God or gods but Kali is of deep importance to her. I have little enough of the woman in me but since coming upon Kali am proud to acknowledge what there is. It is the women of the world who are uncompromising in the battle for renewal. In spite of the skulls, the extended tongue (which I think of as a sign of strength), and the terrible anger, and maybe because of them, Kali is Woman in her true grace.

Against which the effete creature that has evolved out of the need to appeal to men, and is far too much a thing of men's construction, has missed the way. Tagore, as sympathetic to the female character as any male writer, at the end of a sonnet on 'Woman' sums it up: 'Man decorates you, veils you, makes you shy, / till you are precious, hidden, rarefied. / All lit up by his longing, his elation, / you are half woman, half imagination.'

But in the world as it is women are lovely and God knows I find them so. The attachment phenomenon, a form of being in love, covers bands and books, princesses, and goddesses and gods as well. It is this last infatuation which is the most dangerous. Among Hindu deities the lines of identity are not too tight, and between them and their followers can exist a freemasonry of the spirit. They are not alone in this; many Irish are on nodding terms with a saint or saints, or indeed feel a personal friendship with the Virgin Mary; and in a faith where the outward definers are strictest, often an ease abounds. It is the outward ease of the Hindu pantheon I am so struck by. I am taken with these characters of epic, so beautiful and graceful and strong, and ultimately, as one divines, so gentle. If fairy-tales there must be, they are my choice to people the book of romance.

Diana by any standards was a remarkable lady and there is no doubting her passionate concern for landmine victims and for a freeness in the life of children everywhere. If she inspired love, that is not in itself a bad thing. If children, too, read a series of vivid adventures and love doing so – is it a problem? I am caught between different forces, my skull a Kurukshetra, a battleground, where sweeping judgements rule the skies, and simple values fall by the wayside. I have my own cycle of renewal to run, though for me it is all in one life. Characters from the Indian page are real to me as my own blind plot unfolds. Shiva, spouse both of Durga and Kali, has a thunderous significance for me as the god of time, the destroyer, the lord of the dance. But it is Kali, I guess, I am in love with, even though she makes me suffer for it.

Today the sun is born. What terrible
  instant-of-cosmos is touched to flame? Kali
a row of skulls about her neck, makes free
in black and unimaginable anger
to stamp out the mad mind to a first-freshness,
and make a demonised world a lamb again.
Mother of dacoits, drinker of blood at midnight,
I fear you in your stories, I fear the method
that makes fire out of fire, that burns the poor Earth
over and over again, its crazed cracked land
gasping, gasping an ancient forest-word
over and over again, again to burn,
again to be. I fear you in my life
as well. Today I welcome your pure being.

22

The quality of festival enters the home. A family event is often a street event. Certainly it was when I went to a *mukhe-bhat* celebration, that is held when a baby takes solid food for the first time. The extended family occupied every house in the small North Calcuttan lane. It was not well-off but had managed to grow and stay together. At six months for a boy and seven for a girl a little rice or some other food is taken, the first spoonful proffered by someone of the mother's family. (R. had refused to acquiesce in the distinction and P. had had her *mukhe-bhat* at six months, gnawing happily on a bone.) A ceremony at a temple (not in the slightest intrusive) has taken place; it is all a part of the delight. So here I am, in a low room, sitting with a baby boy on my lap, with any number of his relatives grinning down, and I know all about boys, I've had two sons, and I chatter to the infant and he laughs and I rise from the seat to throw him a foot or so into the air to catch him and I haul the body back at the last instant before it leaves my hands and sit down, grinning inanely, and my blood is cold. The whirling four-bladed ceiling fan is lower than I am used to and I was about to project a small head into its path.

No-one seemed to catch on. My behaviour at social gatherings in England has been imperfect at times but to bring a celebration to a close in such a manner ... the sentence won't finish. I don't know how near I really was to letting go of the child, but I do know my blood went cold, or it felt like it, and beneath the cheerfulness of the occasion the memory lingers, an initiation of my own into fear.

Which is always there, I guess, but we walk down the other side of the road without seeing. It was an absurdist reminder, in a way, of the chill hand at the back of it all, an unseen immanence. All about Calcutta, as in any community but somehow carelessly, almost offhandedly, the opposites are let lie, disorder, disease and death, and spontaneous warmth and the richness of ceremonies, and with them an unfrantic making-do, the bare clothes of life. It is amazing there is not more disease when the wet weather comes, as every year the city floods at the drop of a hat, the drains are always blocked, cars plough along in feet of water and people walk knee-deep, waist-deep, chest-deep if need be. At times a phenomenal amount of water will amass in a low-lying area and continue its still possession for days.

Sudder Street, the tourists' hang-out, was prone to a certain swamping, especially at the Hotel Maria entrance. Barefoot, carrying my sandals, I trod on a drowned rat once making my way back in. The complex of roads where I later lived, in Jodhpur Park in the south of the city, was a natural basin and it was there that I had to walk a couple of hundred yards once with the water up to my shoulders. I had an injured thumb and had to get to a medical centre; I kept it clear as I walked, had it seen to, kept it clear back, no trouble. It had rained continuously for three days and nights and the lake lay incongruously over roads and park-ground and round several hundred houses, taking as long again to start going down. When it did subside children caught small fish at the roadside outside my house, though we were far distant from the river. In a village outside Calcutta a friend of mine lived for two weeks on the (flat) roof of his house with his family, including a baby. At one point he had to wade two miles or more, much of it shoulder-deep, to pick up his teacher's salary. No epidemics were reported.

A natural disorder is one thing, however laboriously dealt with; a human another. I came out of the Jodhpur Park flat once to a tumult of shouting. Round the corner, in the main road, a bus was on fire. Two burnt-out bus shells were nearby. In each case driver, conductor and passengers had been forced out and the vehicle set ablaze. A crowd was watching and waiting for the next one. No police were on the scene though a police station was very close; then while I was there about half a dozen police came charging at the crowd with helmets and *lathis* (short thick sticks they are rarely without). We scarpered. They retreated also and three more buses were set alight. A mother and child had been knocked down and killed by a previous bus as they were crossing the road. It is a not uncommon response. The citizenry has no confidence at all in the police to catch the offender (the original driver probably absconded; it's what often happens) or in the courts to punish him. A protest is made, anger fills the sky. As I look back the blazing bus and the two black wrecks in the mild afternoon road shine with a demonic power.

Air, water, fire. While I was still at the Hotel Maria, near the end of my first year, there was a plague scare. It came to nothing; but a piece of advice issued at the time was not to handle a dead rat or to leave one lying around. A few lived at or by the hotel; one slithered under my door there once as I was reading in the middle of the night, rummaged though a bag on the floor, found nothing and slithered out. Now however in the middle of the scare there was one lying in the yard outside the row of 'cells' I was in, clearly dead. I informed the manager. He had a look and yelled for Bullet, the menial on the lowest rung of the staff ladder. Bullet had gone out. No action. After a bit I asked the manager if it could be moved by someone else; after all there was someone around who cleaned the toilets, not that I said that. I was told to wait for Bullet. After a couple of hours I decided to get rid of it myself and approached it with newspaper. To my amazement I was physically prevented from doing anything by two of the staff. Wait for Bullet. After perhaps another hour Bullet turned up and simply picked it up with bare hand and dropped it into a bin. The hotel could relax. The problem foreigner had quietened down and the sacred hierarchy of offices had been preserved.

Images of the city. At the time, of course, one's experience of the place was a more monotonous affair, going here, going there, over cracked pavements, into the dust and dirt that cakes one's fingernails at the end of each day, deeper into a maze and more at home. T.S.Eliot caught something of the personality of London in 'The Waste Land'. Calcutta is less glamorous than London was then, and less glamorous than Calcutta was then, the second city of the Empire, as it was sometimes called. How much better to be itself. My journey into the metropolis was not as hard as Eliot's, my poetry ludicrously plainer, infinitely less resonant, but my affection for the place I walked in and wrote of, perhaps not altogether different from his.

*S*ometimes a clanking dusty harshness
set up stall in the street of my mind.
Where shall I find the drab street's end?
Nowhere is there a drop of freshness.
Over the seas a pavement-poshness
seems as silvery as the wind
whistling down a tinselly land
of shop-front richness, car-seat plushness.

Give me this street with its choking fumes,
this hollowness through which I trek
to the end of the lowered-down sky, it seems.
And though I cough, yet I will speak
of the tug of a street goddess's arms,
Calcutta, and sing a love-song for her sake.

23

Santiniketan is a village unlike any other. A three-hour train ride to the north of Calcutta, in the district of Birbhum, it is often visited by the city-dwellers. Some have second (or first) homes there, some like to go for a day or two when they can; and thousands will go for certain festivals: *Poüs Mela*, *holi*, a famed gathering of Bauls. *Poüs Mela* was instituted by Tagore and belongs to the village, a great fair in late December. *Holi* is everywhere a welcoming of Spring, and in Santiniketan it is carried off with a marvellous freshness, a host of people daubing one another respectfully or not quite so respectfully after quiet solemnities in the open air. It was and still is very much Tagore's village and (it is my fancy) something of his spirit attaches itself to this ceremony of Nature. The occasion has a hint of rebirth to it, a constant in his thoughts as mirrored in his writings; and the enactment among trees that he knew of a stillness of soul and a gala of lightness is apt to call him to mind. The crowds do not go for that (consciously) but it may be why the occasion has blossomed there. The Bauls are a sect of singers and musicians of whom more later. Their songs are searching, rich in image, often accompanied by a driven staccato on a stringed instrument. Their matter is humanist and religious at once; the singer a committed thing. There are other special moments in the year; but people do not come for these only, but, I think, for a refreshment of the spirit that the place offers. Santiniketan means 'abode of peace' and in a wakeful sense it is well named.

It is of course home to many hundreds of people who do not take holiday breaks from the grind of eking out an existence. There are many Santhals, an indigenous tribespeople with their own language, low on the scale of economic indicators and rich in family and community sense, and (as with many Indian tribes) heroic in sustaining it against an inevitable slight current of homogenisation. Their children wander the fields picking up leaves and twigs. Nothing is wasted. Also keeping an eye on the middle class and serving their needs are a few dozen cycle-rickshaw-*wallahs*, stall-owners, and the invisible army of menial workers all layered societies depend on. Tagore's father, the Maharshi, a spiritual leader and prime mover in the creation of the forward-looking Brahmo sect, purchased a patch of land there when it was all a bare stretch as a tranquil haven. Rabindranath later founded a school on it, Patha Bhavan, and a university, Visva Bharati, that continue (the school recently celebrated its centenary). A village naturally grew around them. The place became his second home and his first love. It is still a village of rural and academic concerns, with none of a town's congested anonymity. Despite the wide recognition accorded the two institutions, that are funded by the central government of India rather than the state, something of the Maharshi's concept remains. It is easy to say the school and university are the hub; or that Tagore's presence is greater than any current inhabitant's; but it is not what he would have wished and not of course true. The village people are the hub and all he did was in a sense for any single one among them. What was vital to him was the living individual from the village outward.

It is and it is not Tagore's village then; and after a few visits its air was special for me; I felt attached. And then I was: for I was offered a part-time job there for a year and accepted. I became a Visiting Fellow at Visva Bharati. It sounds grand enough; but they needed someone to sub-edit the Visva Bharati Quarterly which was to be re-issued in English. In addition I taught (at my request) at Patha Bhavan, the school, and started to translate a book of prose poems and short stories by Tagore, 'Lipika'. Apart from once meeting someone's students I had nothing directly to do with the university.

For three days a week now I lived in Santiniketan. My main work was at the school. Lessons are held outside, each class under a tree, except when it rains. The strictures of the national syllabus leave little room for the intentions of the founder to be followed directly, but the symbolic link between Nature and the mind's discovery is kept. And despite the distractions of the outside I found it to be not merely symbolic but to instil something into the pace of teaching and learning that was right. I cannot resist one anecdote. I was told to teach a sonnet of Milton's to a class of fourteen-to-fifteen-year-olds. Syntactically it's the toughest sonnet in the English language; and these were children at a Bengali-medium school whose spoken and read English was unremarkable. 'When I consider how my light is spent / Ere half my days in this dark world and wide,' so far so good. 'And that one talent which is death to hide / Lodged with me useless,' this takes a little time, and I'm praying I haven't ruined the poetry in it for them forever. 'Though my soul more bent / To serve therewith my maker,' we manage to tack this onto the idea of his having something he wants to write. But in the effort I'm enduring (I always do) to keep track of this sentence I may have lost them. 'And present / My true account, lest he returning chide,' well, I'm never sure what 'returning' means. Is it the Day of Judgement? Or is it merely replying, or handing back the unworthy account? Let it be a hint of all of them. And now the main clause of this extraordinary sentence, ' "Doth God exact day-labour, light denied?" / I fondly ask.' Strewth. I'd like Milton to have taught this sonnet under these trees. The rest isn't as compressed and they appreciate the final line, in which Patience tells the young writer not to fret. 'They also serve who only stand and wait.' I tell them of another sonnet of his, again touching on his blindness, when he is dreaming of his dead wife and then, 'But O as to embrace me she inclined / I waked, she fled, and day brought back my night.' It isn't all wasted. But the vagaries of inapposite syllabus poem-selection aren't confined to the UK.

I loved teaching there. The pupils called me Joe-da, and wrote many memorable poems and poem-snippets themselves, often of details of what they saw and felt around them, caught in image. In my flat, lent by the university and in dire need of repair, I read weird and wonderful articles from academics around the globe that must have failed to be published anywhere else. Visva Bharati seemed ready to accept them all. There was a list of only fourteen addresses to which the journal was sent. There is something about university life that I have never been able to fathom. Tagore refused to take a degree (though he accepted an Oxford D.Litt. in old age). He intended the academy he started to have higher standards. "Visva Bharati acknowledges India's obligation to offer to others the hospitality of her best culture and India's right to accept from others their best." But I should say in fairness that some articles were good, and that the university had outstanding musical and art departments; and that I have a blind spot about universities anyway. My translation work kept me engaged otherwise and I got to know a number of characters about the place, a cycle-rickshaw-*wallah* called Arun, and a lady everyone called Didi ('elder sister') who ran a tea-and-toast stall and who sang an enchanting song once, about oranges (*kamala-lebu*) in a soft light voice, out of keeping with her generous frame. And the place itself, that I used to explore in the long still afternoons, for school started and stopped early, and there was a hush in the land, and one could venture into its heart, merely by walking.

U nseen because so common, all these lives
     of leaves and grass-stem, tree-wood, flapping cow's-ears,
questioning dog's-tails, bird-wing, and a citizenry
at home in green, of yellow white red blue.
So common that it stays unheard, a remark
of individual nature. And the broad
discussion of the streets, the parliament-houses,
roars past on a dead-set arterial highway,
to drown the note and blur the sight. This issue
is the green leaf of all. Now in the air
about a village-path, the sound of bells.
Down long flowering tree-fingers, and struck
by all life's quietness, I hear it ring,
the poetry of the day, in Santiniketan.

24

"Garam deem! Garam deem! Chai, chai, chai! Paper! Paper! Biscoot! Biscoot! Biscoot! Coffee! Coffee!" At Bardhaman Junction, on the way to Santiniketan, the train is invaded by voices. Hot boiled eggs, tea, newspapers, biscuits, coffee, a charged clattering chorus of calls. High and low, instinctively in rhythm, a few bars of pure symphony. Male vendors old and young have boarded the train before it stopped and will not leave till it is moving again, sometimes conducting a sale including fishing out change as the train gathers speed and nonchalantly stepping off with heavy tray onto the end of the platform. Later, as we near Bolpur (the nearest station to the village), a Baul will sing songs of a quiet seeking and yearning, if he is the one I always look forward to. I alight from the Santiniketan Express with the grey world of the metropolis far behind me. The husk of the journey is gone; and something is left over, like a remainder, as I make my way to school.

Nor is the situation so different now. All Indian journeys are tiring. But with mine over I take with me a seed of refreshment. I would not care to extend the idea to the journey we all undertake, though a religious person will; and one can feel the attraction.

It may be no more than a by-product of getting on in years; but I think living in India, including an acquaintance of a sort with Tagore's works and personality, has attuned me to a vibrancy of inner thought, if one may use the term, that is as old as the hills. If so I am grateful for the speck of understanding.

Including, too, an acquaintance with one or two remarkable women. In Santiniketan I met Trina Purohit Roy, who had returned fairly recently from thirty-five years in Germany. She had set up an institution in the village that is about as uninstitutional as you can get, to offer a healing care to whoever may come. Local children sing, play instruments and engage with some of the academic basics on the floor of her sitting-room every day. When young she was a notable musician. In Germany she had a baby boy who was severely brain-damaged a few days after birth. (A nurse may have dropped him; it was never clear.) After seeing the mechanical efforts of officialdom to attend to the child's needs she took his care wholly into her hands. He was blind, had epileptic fits, and very little prospect of any kind of life at all. By trial and error she felt her way to a musical therapy for him that worked wonders. When I met Bapi, about forty, sitting in his chair (he could not walk but could see perfectly), he greeted me by echoing my name with pleasure, giving the word the same weighting that I had. He loved musical sounds, and would sit in front of a keyboard all day touching the notes lightly at random. He enjoyed people's company immensely, often laughing delightedly, especially with the children around. Trina-di (a familiar and respectful suffix for an older woman) extended a thoughtful care to everyone, a mix of humour and practicality and intuitive understanding; and Bapi sat there, and sits there, the unconscious key to it all. They could have stayed in Germany but she chose to return home, with little money, and set up what amounts to an ashram. A large rat came in one evening when the children were singing, looked around in an undisturbed fashion, and was gone. Chetanalok (the name of the organisation), 'awareness-people/place/light', has a welcome for one and all.

It certainly had one for me. Trina-di helped me word by word with my translation of 'Lipika', the volume of Tagore's prose I had taken on, both on the first time through and in a finely detailed discussion of the completed draft. She took infinite pains (but no money); and while her English was good she often could not quite find the words to say why something of mine jarred. Her sense of English was uncanny and I trusted her ear; and so we both had to exercise some patience. I found I regarded the situation as a teacher-disciple one: a surprise as I had thought myself unable to submit to a senior presence such as that of a guru. I hasten to add she did not see it like that. She helped me in the early mornings in Santiniketan and I would often visit her later in the day, the children there, and never leave without a sense of wholeness.

She continues in old age to give and to receive. I think what I have taken from knowing her is a possibility, a trust in the universe that allows one, despite all disappointments, to open the door wide. It is not a possibility I want to take up, but to continue to know of. It is presumptuous but I would say of her life, it is the most beautiful one I have known.

There was another lady who meant more to me. Gauri Ayyub was the headmistress of the school referred to earlier, Khelaghar, House of Play, that I taught at on Sundays for a time. She had inherited a terrible degenerative arthritis that had crippled her in her mid-sixties. When I met her she was capable of directing meetings of the school staff, propped on a couch, but the disease soon went beyond that. We used to talk at great length and I read to her as she lay in bed, Thomas Mann's 'The Magic Mountain'. We got halfway through. When she died R. and I went and sat in her room for an hour or two by the dead body (that she had donated for organ use), in company with relations and friends.

Someone said she was a human being in a trillion, and (not taken literally) it did not sound wrong. Though it is the least important thing, she was preternaturally intelligent. Once I read to her a translation of mine of one of Tagore's poems (from the 'Gitanjali'). She was lying flat in bed, unable even to hold a piece of paper let alone a book. She asked me to repeat the middle verse (of three); I did; and then she quoted the original second verse line by line in the Bengali and my translation for each phrase, to show me what I was missing. She had married a professor twenty-five years her senior (who had passed away some time before) and had a life-destroying falling-out with her father on account of it. Not because her husband was older, but because he was a Muslim. That he was a colleague of her father's (they were professors of philosophy at the same university) was neither here nor there. During the war with Pakistan that led to the emergence of the nation of Bangladesh she had run a network of safe houses in Calcutta for refugees on the run; and time after time she had gone out to flooded villages in West Bengal with blankets and food. But this for me was not the important thing either. She had a gift of knowing people. R. felt it too. My translation of the 'Gitanjali' came out as she died and I dedicated it 'to Gauri Ayyub of Calcutta'. Where she lived there was a small metal foundry down the road and all day the hammering of metal came through the window. She said once they were hammering on the side of her head; and in the same breath, that they had to make a living. People made their lives out of her. At the end she lay in great pain for many days. When R. and I left the room where the body rested I did not know if it was an acceptable thing to do or not but I went to her side and touched her warm cheek. I only knew her at the end of a pain-torn journey; but her warmth stays in that touch. There is a seed of refreshment that stays over from a life, but it is carried on not to a next world, but in the lives of other people in this.

*D*own the dead weeks a body floats. Survival
is its weak point: the breath goes on and on,
but all the play of the forest-life is gone.
Exhaustedness, a sense of near-arrival;
and hints of darkness now. In the lee of the wall
it drifts relentlessly, abandoning all.
Medicine pays a phantom call. Revival –
that murderous path – is not embarked upon.
The forest play was beautiful. If Nature
gave all its love and quickness to one creature,
to gift to all – would it not light the future,
a day that danced with Nature's festival?
But pain has chosen too. A body lying
in Beckbagan, for all. A woman dying.

25

Death as a concept has its freedom where there is nowhere to hide. In the West we are a tad insulated. Its implicit presence adds a loveliness to some of India's art, and not least, in my view, to the songs of the Bauls. Full of a passionate yearning, sometimes wistful, sometimes savage, a racing of the blood on the air, it is the music of Life not Death they are charged with; and the thinking of the Bauls as expressed apart from their songs is in part a revel in the colourfulness of Being. But Life would not be so strong if Death were not there too. Often their songs tell of the Person of the Heart, who has all the appeal in the world for me; for the singers are godless.

They are a centuries-old sect who know of the soul (often it is a bird) but not of a god or gods. Bengal is their home, and Santiniketan and the area about, a nerve-centre; they are part of the place and it of them. Tagore was inspired by them. A Baul song is a poem in its use of image, which (if not always original) leaves a telling impression on the mind. Thousands of streamlets of pure folk-art, arising from a life-style that is committed, distinctive, and simple in demand, irrigate the Indian land. It is a place to be in the open air.

I am in Kalor Dokan. It is like a village square, but more enclosed and uneven, an informal meeting-point in Santiniketan. The name, Kalo's Shop, is of an old and celebrated tea-house at one side, and now of the place too. There is a basic restaurant and one or two shops and offices round about. No-one sits inside to eat or drink anything. There is no inside. In the afternoon I often go and sit under a tree sipping black tea, 'liquor cha' (after the colour). No alcohol is on sale. The idea is unthinkable. Students at the university get a cheap lunch; and in the evening the place is full, people drifting in on bikes and the odd motorbike. It is a place of *adda*, conversation, being together; and also of being not alone, but in a kind of *adda* of presences. It's as if the pace of Santiniketan, which is in a sense that of everyone's diurnal round, unrushing and unceasing, is a tangible thing as one sits there in the deserted late afternoon. For me it becomes a place to touch base, so to speak; and whether on my own or caught up in heated debate, to have an ally under the stars.

Everybody has a place where they feel welcome. Or they should have. Kalor Dokan let me be; instead of a civilisation pawing at you, it has a rough-and-ready ease. One afternoon I was surprised to see the youth who had threatened me in my Park Street flat, the one with a dangerous air of not being in control, clearing the tables there. He was working as a cook in the restaurant. We talked a little guardedly. There was no reference to the previous incident, now behind us. He seemed to be doing all right. It was an unexpected meeting, but not out of place.

I cycled a lot in Santiniketan. The long narrow road that leads through the village is haunted by cyclists, often in clusters, students chatting gaily, children (the odd small boy on a woman's bike, too small to sit on the saddle but manfully pedalling away), roaming youngsters, a few of the middle-aged or elderly. All share the road with any number of pedestrians, the occasional car, bus, lorry, the atoms flowing around one another effortlessly. At night no cycle has a light at front or back. Still students coast up and down the long road gossiping, their night-sight far better than mine. I had a few wild and wonderful moments, once crashing into a bridge and almost into the canal, as I forgot the road curved right there; and once in the total black-out of an overcast night groping my way home down countless avenues thick with hedges and hedge-life, till I found the right one. After some months I started to hold a small torch, as I should have done from the outset. One of my finest memories is cycling a few miles late at night to visit friends in a neighbouring village, or returning from them, under the brilliant stars.

I rented a room from an elderly couple for a time after the Fellowship-plus-flat came to an end, as I often returned to the village. My host, Mr Banerjea, still took his bike out on a short daily excursion, though he was suffering a certain loss of understanding and ability to engage with the world around him. He was a gentle soul and a gentleman, who has now passed away. His wife too is no longer with us, my hostess, sharp of mind and deaf of ear, whose hearing aids succeeded in emitting a constant series of whistles but in little else. Mrs Banerjea, a tender soul, always busy in the house, stays in my mind incongruously like the bougainvillaea in her lovely garden. Admitted into more than the use of a room I count it a rare privilege to have met this fragile, hardy couple, though I did not know them well.

Once returning at night to their house R. and I stepped over a long snake lying across the drive. Neither head nor tail was visible. I was about to step on it when R. stopped me. Snakes are a feature of life in Santiniketan especially when the rains come, but I saw hardly any; they tended to see me first. A couple of times from the seat of a cycle-rickshaw I was aware of an instant of black whirl at the side of the road. I heard various stories of cobras including one in the university flat next to mine. But though I half-hoped for it I didn't see one myself. And in all honesty the stories sufficed.

I spent a lot of time in the evenings in the porch of my flat. It had a separate door onto the outside with bars instead of a front wall and I kept my bike within the protected space, barely leaving room for a chair and myself. A painting formed in my mind of the back wheel of the bike with all the spokes radiating from the hub set against the vertical iron bars. Beyond is an aura of grass, trees; but the metallic construction is the picture's exclamatory fact, a large three-quarters wheel within bars filling the canvas, a hint of ironwork tracery to the side on a wall. It says something I want to say, and it can be left said in the picture.

Not that I ever tried to paint it. The same has happened a few other times in my life and each picture is complete and stored in my mind. My actual handling of a paintbrush is so disastrous it might as well be tied to my elbow. There was another in Santiniketan. I used to walk miles along a canal path and once as I came down to it paused to watch a herd of cows move along it and across a road and continue on the path the other side. They would have been on a two- or three-day journey to a cattle fair. Two cowherds were in attendance and one of them is in the picture, together with some of his charges and the canal and road in the late afternoon. He is about twenty, has bare feet and ragged clothes, and the body of a splendid athlete. He has no idea of this and stands, stick in hand, in front of the great animals as they cross. The painting is called 'The Olympian'. All my pictures are of something I've seen and I would give the world to see them effected, but at least they hang in the gallery of my mind. These two are no more than footnotes to a companionship with a place, that countless others have had and will have, each in their own way.

India has let me discover a little of myself, and nowhere more than Santiniketan. The canal path was a good place to be on one's own. Often I revisit for a moment the open vistas of countryside there, and the sparse woodland at the side.

*S*uch silent people speak so silently
    along the path of eucalyptus trees,
such shadows group together, tree by tree
of winding, tall, leaf-clustering presences
from an older time, it seems to me, that these
whose stately gossip is unheard, may be
a hint of Nature down the centuries,
a word to the wise; and that they speak to me.
And I can only listen, not divine
a word to tell. I step on gnarled root-plinths
and look beyond, at water-hyacinths
and at slow-moving cattle, for a sign;
and back and up, into the topmost trees.
I shall become as almost-still as these.

26

R. and I were going through a bad patch. She was not yet living with me and neither of us knew quite what we wanted. She had been trying to get a divorce for years, from before we met, and the process kept stalling. Because of where she had lived with her husband (and still lived after throwing him out for continued mental and physical abuse) the case was handled by a district court outside Calcutta, that was unutterably dilatory in its workings. She would make the long journey to find it shut as someone was ill; or because there'd been a commotion at it the week before. Or else it would be open and her husband absent and the next part of the hearing shelved yet again. He would be fined a paltry few rupees for not turning up and so it dragged on. He had told her he would do all he could to obstruct the proceedings. The judge attached to the case was known to be conservative in outlook and unsympathetic to the woman's side. As indeed the law was: a divorced woman's right to care for her child could be desperately hard to establish, and even if granted, she could expect no financial support. R. was concerned with the first point; and while P. was adamant she would stay with her mother and the child's voice was to be heard, it was by no means a foregone conclusion. One needed a liberal judge which it appeared R. did not have. Her association with me was not going to help matters. At one point her husband put a detective agency onto any female visitor I had; they were followed home and quizzed about their relationship with me. Any dirt he could drag up he would. All this added to the uncertainty that lay between us.

But it did give us a shared cause. It took a long time, two changes of lawyer, and a judge's retirement, but when the case finally went through the result was the right one. By that time we had set up together, moved, become a couple; and about three months after the decree we married. But there had been much to work through or round or to evade, a destructive emptiness at core, gradually to be occupied by the business of living together. Time after time a dangerous vacuum drew us in. Without going into a profitless discussion of forces within us on either side, in any case outside our proper understanding, there was in each I think a remnant of hollowness, left over from childhood letdown, that made trust difficult. It was during one such rocky episode that we found ourselves, ironically enough, on holiday in the state of Himachal Pradesh in the Himalayas.

On the way we stopped in Simla, the famous hill station, and walking in the evening found ourselves looking at the array of lights flung up and down the hillside, and knowing we were thinking the same thing. Human habitation, here and strange, stretching on and on. She said "Why?" and

I said nothing. For a short time we were as close as we have been. Later that evening we had a furious argument about nothing at all. I was bewildered, she was angry, we continued our journey.

We reached Manali, our destination, and it was the same. We could not return for two weeks as the train tickets were for a certain day; and fiercely co-existed, immeasurably distant, in a small room playing cards. And there were moments of togetherness than which nothing is finer. One morning we set out to climb a hill to a cave where a hermit lived. Leaving the road we started the climb and soon saw it was a tougher proposition than we had realised. R. walks slowly and has relatively small lungs that make ascent difficult. In addition we could see it was going to be a hit-or-miss affair: no signs or clear path and only a general direction to go by. I asked her if she thought she could do it and she gave a cloud-breaking smile and said "Let's try". We took our time and found it. I seem less geographically confused in the freedom of the hills than on low-lying earth; at any rate I made a couple of lucky guesses, and there we were. The journey down continued the mood of simple beauty within and without. Soon the ugliness returned.

The hermit had left wife and daughters in the town some twenty years before and holed up in the cave, now widely known. He made the occasional short foray down. It is acceptable to give up responsibilities for a holy calling, that it is taken for granted such a departure is. R. talked to him while I sat outside, later suffering for it, and wrote a poem. Sitting there with the noon sun blazing on my bare head I did not notice it. The snowcapped mountains, the river nearby that I could not see, the light clouds cradled me, and something in me seemed to come to a decision. But it was not the one I thought.

The holiday continued worse and worse. When we finally caught our train we didn't speak to each other for two days, and on reaching Howrah Station in Calcutta simply split up. R. walked out of the station faster than I had ever seen her move. She went home to her flat in Salt Lake, I to mine in Park Street, it was over. I was due to visit England almost at once: I went, came to terms with what had happened, and returned in a month, independent-minded, ready to carry on on my own.

And went to see R. She was lying in bed in her flat which had an eviction notice nailed to the door. The block was officially for government workers, in this case minor clerical staff and the like attached to municipal offices. After many years it was being claimed as such. She was recovering from an operation. There was no animosity in the meeting. I asked her to come and live with me. She said she would.

The poem-decision had been the one after all that I had come to. Or it had come to me. Outside the hermit's cave I had felt in the hand of Nature. For all its nightmarish side, for me the holiday also had been a great gift.

We never really talked about what had happened, and did not need to. In any case we couldn't; whatever force had been at work was a disturbing one, past words. Before the holiday we had at times talked about living together but it had seemed too much of a step. In addition it played into the hands of R's husband; for while she was still officially married to him, such a move was likely to predispose the judge in his favour. But it was time to stop beating about the bush and we both knew that. Sometimes a disturbance is needed, though I would not wish on anyone the storm of the psyche that visited us. Now I see the sun breaking through that I could not then (except in R.'s smile). More, at a distance in time of some ten years I see the mysterious hand of Nature, working by opposites, ready to yield up a freshness. The Himalayas, home of ice, are God-given: it is the only word, though it has no meaning. Our trouble is we use too many words, and try and find a meaning for them all.

What can speak louder than these silences,
  this sage white-splendid council, at whose feet
the world goes on part-lost, never to meet
itself, to cut across its distances?
What can speak louder than this force of night,
a white mane thundering over a thirsty land,
crying out with the charge of Nature's command,
dimmed into dreams, forgotten in daylight?
What can speak louder than the softest of sails
that search and search not as they go above
in infinite quiet upon the deepest of seas?
High on a hill in Himalayan breeze
something has spoken in me, though my voice fails.
Here in the Kulu valley I know my love.

27

There is a freshness in the Himalayas that is also a freshness of thought. A resonant silence calls on the mind to listen. 'Hills deep in meditation' Tagore called them, and they seem to have been associated forever with a journey to discovery. Countless individuals have gone there to be and to think, and still go, for months at a time, sometimes longer. There is a mountain in Japan visited by those with the same austere purpose. How far that country is affected by a perspective from the high spots I have no idea; but India is in part possessed by what one may call its hill-thinking. It is not a solemn matter, but one of lightness, or light; and in a diffuse but real way, it has cast a spell over the land.

The insights of the ancient Vedic texts owe something to the Himalayan summons, maybe a good deal. A pilgrimage to the holy lake at Kailash, say, is also at a certain level a paying of respect to the intellectual tradition of the land, however formally uneducated the traveller may or may not be. Wherever one is in India, one is not altogether cut off from the far past; and a mountain presence harbours the soul.

This is to put it fancifully, perhaps, but it may approximate to something one cannot say prosaically. At any rate, however much an outsider, I feel the speck of Indian identity I may have acquired to be nourished by the mighty range. To revisit even in memory is momentarily to still a yearning that is at once nebulous and deep. In its way it is a kind of pilgrimage.

Unfortunately one memory that can return in vivid clarity is a slightly appalling one. Out walking, I gained the end of a green rise to look down at a stream: and saw a vast shock of plastic bags littering the long bank. Thousands of them of different colours; a discarding-spot the locals may have regarded even with civic pride, as at least they were in the same place. An abrupt reminder of day-to-day living.

There were others. Women breaking stones at the roadside with small hammers, earning eight rupees (then about 15p.) for several hours' work, breathing in the dust. Women carrying down great bundles of wood from the forest on their backs. The road they were walking down was good enough for a small lorry; but nobody in the village below was going to set up the necessary operation, though it may quickly have provided more jobs for those laid off. Women are there so use them. And cripple them. Once walking down a long country road in another time and place, between two villages in Rajasthan, I saw approaching from far off two figures. It was a hot interminable afternoon, no-one else was in sight, for some time I was not sure if the two figures were moving or standing still. Then I made out they were two women who did indeed seem to be coming my way; but why so slowly? When finally we passed I saw why. They had heavy rings of burnished metal on their ankles. A sign of marriage. The scene is symbolic for me of something insane in the treatment of women across the globe. It's little different in a quiet Himalayan village; and only as a matter of degree, anywhere else.

One is often distracted by such memories, and the need to rant; but what I would like to do, as this account passes the mid-point, is somehow to find a path in words to an idea India and the Himalayas have left me with. The idea is of a state of being, a freshness, in which one can go ahead and things get done; and the Gordian knot at the root of the consciousness is let be. In which a clarity attends the workings of the individual, and of the community, that lets us see more easily beyond ourselves, and the species, to cosmic fact as we know it. This is in a handful of stones as much as in the Milky Way. An alertness, and an increasing co-operativeness with the forces of Nature, are our birthright: and the art of living can be pursued more finely than as yet we have commonly known.

A ready objection from our standpoint now is on the lines of, "And will there ever be a 'Hamlet' written in this brave new world of yours?" To which the answer is, "A 'Hamlet' for the times, with all the darkness and the pain, the wrongheadedness and the heroism, the ambiguities and the humour of the greatest of Shakespearian plays. But the princely character of later times will discover an entanglement we cannot know now or see." Art will have its vision and some will be bleak. But we will be operating on a wider, more generous, and at the same time more accurate level. In art as in other matters an acuity related to living need will increase.

It's just an idea, a leap forward in perception that I feel is waiting for us, and has been waiting a long time in the compelling Indian hills. Psychological insights in the old Sanskrit texts are no less remarkable than the parochial views of right and wrong that they are embedded in: the loyalty to a form of words rather than to their spirit; the caste system, the parade of power, the ostentatious ego. Society is holding us back but the hills are there to take us forward. And in my petty life a few visits to some of their lower reaches have led me, however misguidedly, at least to be able to have a vision.

Shiva, the god of creation and destruction, lives at Kailash. It is a paradox I have not yet come to terms with that the three senior deities, Brahma, Vishnu and Shiva, are all male, and yet the female divine character is as vivid and free as they. Parvati is Shiva's wife of the mountains: she is also Durga, and Kali, but more lovely in a feminine way. I found myself thinking of the couple as I walked in the low highlands. It was not word-thinking so much as child-thinking, a being close; and inevitably I felt my city-soul, that seems to have spent its life in a stranglehold, go back to something like its early days. I used to walk for miles in Cornwall on little errands, before the age of five, and later to cycle in Buckinghamshire lanes for many hours on my own in the afternoon and evening, all before the onset of war at secondary school. Waged not so much by the other boys as by the system, it defeated the puny individual that I was on the very first day. If the land's openness is on a sufficient scale something of an early freedom is returned, as I have found later in Britain and memorably on a trip to Africa. High up it's a different matter again.

It was in the 'hills deep in meditation' that I took a true leave of infancy, in the Indian terms of this account. The foregoing musings, on a quickening of the human element, may seem as if I also took leave of my senses there; but they come from no more than a wish to tease out a lingering intimation. The midway significance is an indulgence on my part. Of more direct relevance to the account is that I left the region surer-footed, with a knowledge I did not know I had, but that is legible now. I knew R. and I could be together. I knew I could write of India. I knew that next to the Earth one is not alone. I had a clearer vision of the past and the bare beginnings of a sense for the future. I knew of a clarity and an openness at the heart of things, and an energy too.

*D*id you know there was a lost boy-child
of the hills? If Shiva and Parvati
knew in their love-making the precarious issue
of stars and water; then in the human world
an undiscovered child had Time to play with;
did you know in old Manali village
he is sometimes here? His body is out of rock
his face is the earth his foot the tree and his touch
is out of snow. His laugh is a far sky-song.
India a mother you have held me close
and today I am weaned. A companion of the hills
breathes into me his words of poetry.
And all of you made out of stars and water,
you have a hill-companion. Did you know?

28

I began to translate another Bengali poet, Jibanananda Das. An Indian forename has a meaning (the surname indicates caste), and for a personality such as his the rare one he was given could scarcely have been less apposite. Yet for the hidden spark beneath the troubled current of his poems, scarcely more. Jibanananda was a withdrawn, self-effacing, rather gloomy person who could seem, from the outside, not so much to live as to haunt his existence. He lived from 1899 to 1954 and I talked with a number of people who had known him. Not by design: it's the way it happens in Calcutta. Everyone interested in literature seems to belong to an unofficial family, a network of recollection and anecdote and inherited memory, that can make a departed writer into a not-so-distant relation. Before I read any of his work I was fascinated by the sense of the man I had gathered.

Jiban is life, *ananda* joy. One often refers to an eminent person in India by the forename, and with a writer whose works live on the usage itself becomes an indication of greatness. It is a wonderful intimacy. Why should not a country take to its heart a true poet, and by the simplest means let everyone be on close terms, a brother or sister?

Rabindranath ('brightest of suns') and Jibanananda, the two indisputably great Bengali poets of the last century, are part of the Bengali family. It is a special reservation within the kinship of the tongue that any writer would surely be glad of, if they could but know it. But 'glad' is not a word that applies to Jibanananda.

A contemporary called him the 'loneliest poet'. He was a natural solitary, on the surface often ill at ease, and able in his writing to come to a reconciliation with life's mazy forces, so that a seer's beauty touches his lines. After he died an exercise-book was found with sixty-two sonnets dated twenty years previously, to which his brother gave the name (a phrase from one of them) 'Rupasi Bangla'. 'The Beautiful Woman, Bengal', almost 'Bengal My Lovely', the sequence quickly became famous. It is no less than a love-poem to the land. He would drift from village to village, or stand or sit for hours by a ragged banyan-tree, or a ruined shrine, or the broken shell of a fallen bird's egg, and let his thoughts gather into a remarkable fourteen lines of one sentence, with many long drifting phrases, and a perfectly-observed Petrarchan rhyme-scheme. The past and the present run together with drifting mind-glimpses of mythical or historical figures, and maybe a woman washing rice, or a girl gathering fruit, and birds, leaves, trees, grass in their passionate presence, and a sense of time and the moment, an indefinable yearning.

A thrill in the air of the richness and individual stamp of Nature seems to meet human sensibilities halfway, the one informing the other, so that rural Bengal itself breathes the restlessness of the writer's musings, and he its peace. As the poems settle in the mind a sense of belonging, and of transience, in an ordinary setting of great beauty, gains a hold. Almost to weep is sometimes the only response. As I translated them I found myself in touch with an empathy for the Earth I did not know existed in tangible form.

Five volumes of his verse were published in his lifetime. Urban themes beat a hammer in the brain. Das was a modernist in style, one of the first; his work reflects the crowding-in of existentialist pressures, the old gods gone. But he does not turn his back on beauty. For me he is the truest of the moderns – for the freshness of the vision of the urban intellectual, so often imitative; and for his refusal to bury his head in the incomplete, the ugly and the bizarre, even as he is subjected to the living shock head-on.

I think his finest single poem is '1946-47'. 'Partly fuelled by the horrors surrounding Partition, the creation of Pakistan out of India at the time of Independence, partly by the writer's sense of the ordinary people of Bengal,' if the reader will forgive my quoting myself again, in 135 lines it gets at the runaway haste of the modern age, the current atrocity committed in blindness and the permanent one; and at the end sees two darknesses, one denying and one, at last, soothing. Somehow the long whispering lines take us from one to the other. 'For a statement of its length it can rarely have been surpassed in the range of its knowing and seeing. I wonder if there is a poem in any language composed since the end of the Second World War that can stand beside it.'

Jibanananda is dearly loved in West Bengal and in

Bangladesh, where he was born when it was East Bengal and geographically, where his rural poetry is located. One reason is his personality, that ironically is so accessible. There is nothing superhuman about him; it is the reverse that one is drawn to, the man in an unhappy marriage, who endured spells of unemployment in an erratic career (he was a lecturer in English at various colleges), and spells of depression, and wrote with a penetration and a vision to take the breath away.

He was a fiction-writer too. A character he often uses can be seen as the figure behind the poems, made more visible. A passive, shadowy, alert presence, scarcely more than a pair of eyes, flickering from this situation to that. In Tagore's wake he laid a new track for the travelling consciousness to follow. As a young man he sent the senior poet a few poems, unfortunately before his style coalesced and (as they say) he found his voice. Tagore, who was in any case anti-modernist, wrote back commending a pictorial quality. One wonders if he saw some of the great pieces that Das produced in the 'thirties and what he may have made of them. Quite likely not very much. Das is often tortuous, and explores areas that Tagore finds no need to. They knew each other little; but any Bengali who reads, virtually, is close to them both.

They present an extraordinary succession, and a legacy to present-day readers of Bengali that surely is second to none. With one there is a deep, far-reaching, and sometimes violent flame. With the other an erratic spark is struck as if from a stone. But if one waits for it there is nothing brighter.

There is more to come of Jibanananda Das. With Rabindranath Tagore he made my stay in Calcutta the privilege of a lifetime. The elder has a treasured place in one's heart, almost a holy one; but one is of the same substance as the younger. Once I was caught in a dust-storm, metaphorically. I couldn't see what I was doing, I was suffocated by my own lethargy, shaken by self-disgust, and then whatever it was let go of me. And whatever it was was nothing to do with India, but rather of me, an incomplete social animal, pitched on the stones, scrabbling a miserable path in no direction. Choked by what is unsatisfactory in the self, unable to beat it back, wanting to hide. It happened outside my Park Street flat one afternoon. For some moments I was the prisoner of a demon. But what freed me was certainly an Indian phenomenon.

L ost on a road that disappears in dust
       I turn, and even in turning lose my way.
Dust-pillows rise to meet me. As if day
were night I sleep; and sink beneath a crust
of hard fact, to half-dream. The slightest gust
of day's air stays about my face, to play
my life's debt-song as if on holiday ...
my sloth, and my false friendship, and my lust.
And so one afternoon I sat outside
lost and ready to cry for life's mistake,
and did not cry but tried again to hide.
And then the world dropped by for friendship's sake,
a sudden wind blew warm on every side –
the monsoon stormed – and I was clean awake.

29

Grass. Jibanananda was one with it. It surged about him and upon him, intermingling its being with his, simply his country's grass, the green loveliness of Bengal. Sometimes he would write of lying under it in death, or within it at rest. Trees, wild flowers, bushes, creepers, all grew individually to his eye. Sights, sounds, smells merge in an exquisite taste and touch of the naked mind and all, too, are separate. The colours of the sky, and especially of the austere months, with their fog and mist, tinge the backcloth of the stage of his poems. And in the foreground the unkempt green.

Until coming to India the only poetic lines I knew of on grass were Wordsworth's, in a passage beginning 'Ye motions of delight, that haunt the sides / of the green hills ...' It's a marvellous moment, the more so for the mystery not being named. And it's a Western moment in which the human animal stands apart from Nature. Wordsworth discovered the depths of interfusion of Nature in the child, the child in the man. Still it is an ordered universe with man in his place. This is Das on grass. 'The Earth is filled

with soft green light this dawn / as if of a lemon-tree's new
leaves; / deer's teeth gnash the green grass as if they tore at
/ unripe pomelos – that's the fragrance – / and I too long
to drink the grass-smell in / like emerald wine, glass after
glass of it. / To sift and churn the grass-mass – to scratch
my eyes / against its eyes – my feathers upon its wing; / to
be born as grass in grass, from some deep grass-mother's /
womb descending in delectable darkness.'

In the original too it lacks the lyrical sweep of the
English poet. But the Bengali words are finely sown with
their own meditative song. Jibanananda allowed his mind
to hearken to the whisper of reincarnation, in his poetry,
but not in the orthodox way. Yet the violence of union with
the elements and the inclusiveness of continuation are very
much part of the land around him. I live and breathe India
in Jibanananda's words.

Insects fly and flutter in his lines, as beautiful as
birds. Townspeople feature: there's a wonderful portrait
of beggars at a roadside in 'Idle Moment'. Written
whimsically it gets inside the heads of a casual threesome
like nothing on Earth. Issues trivial and mortal possess
them. At once it is fiercely funny and fiercely serious. Like
all Das's extraordinary creations, it has the tang of reality.

Which is why, I suppose, the mythic element is so
captivating. A river called Dhansiri winds beneath the
poetic stage like a dream. It is fact and fancy, to be found
in his home district of Bengal and as a familiar of his
poems. An elusive goddess, here and there held for an
instant, light and everlasting.

Always there is something refreshing. The style can be
taxing, the way through a poem parlous, but it is as if in the

barren waste of a world, a well of the clearest water is to be found. It can be argued that the movement of a modernist work of art is to discern a journey of such a nature and its end. No-one has traced its pathway like Das.

The six-year-old girl I played Snakes and Ladders with became my daughter. It happened gradually. Once, before we all lived together, I said to her that I might be her father some day and she put her hands over her ears. When we became a family unit the tenuous bond between the two of us, that already she understood as well as I did, and that partakes in some way of a great love, took on its guarantee so to speak, and all it had to do was to grow. She was at that time at boarding school in Calcutta, and was occasionally visited there by her actual father. It was a difficult situation that she handled wonderfully well.

I tried to let him know that I would never get in the way of his seeing his daughter and wrote him a letter to that effect, doing what I could to express goodwill. He did not answer but handed the letter to his lawyer as ammunition against R. in the divorce case. I went to see him but he turned down any meeting. He proceeded to blacken R.'s name at P.'s school with the result that she was told she had to stop being a boarder and could continue only as a day-girl. She, R. and I accepted the diktat with delight. We had been unwilling to take the risk of her living with us day in and day out, apart from the holidays; but it was the natural thing, though it happened unnaturally. When a year or two later, the divorce case still dragging on, P. went to another school, the deputy headmistress of the old one sneered at her: "Boarder – day-girl – nothing." Initially in the new school too she received vicious treatment at the hands of the management.

It is worth recording. It was a fine institution, Calcutta International School, at which I was already teaching part-time. The headmistress there knew the situation and suggested P. took the entrance exam. P. failed the Maths the first time, excelling in the English, and was invited to re-take. At the age of twelve she demanded the Maths syllabus for the exam, worked intensively on what was by far her worst subject, and passed the re-take with flying colours. The new headmistress named the day for her to start and she was formally withdrawn from the previous school. But the chairman of the board of governors of the new one decided that as her mother appeared to be living in sin with a Westerner the school should not take her; and the headmistress refused to face him down, telling me she would have to return to the old school.

The hypocrisy and cowardice in this were shocking. There are always some unconventional home situations in the background of a school population and neither of these schools was any different. The chairman was an ambitious politico and no-one dared cross him. P. spent three months at home, before the one governor of the new school who was concerned for her, and I, put together a plan that would appeal to the school board's need, which was essentially to assert a petty power. I wrote the board a letter saying that I would not appear at any kind of meeting as her parent or accompany her to or collect her from school and so on. It did the trick and she started, a term missed; and loved the school and did very well there.

Of course the conditions of the letter were ignored from

day one and no-one minded. Power had been exercised in an Indian way. It was an immensely straining three months for all three of us. I continued to teach there, not wanting to lose any goodwill there might be. Once she started it was all put behind us.

As I have said when the divorce finally went through it was entirely in R.'s favour. P. withstood a two-hour cross-examination at court, in her early teens, quite admirably. She saw her actual father only once after leaving the first school (not looking his way at court). She had written to him requesting a meeting and they chatted amicably enough but his pride was such that it was the last time. She was not at all sorry. Since then I have been her father in actuality and, as every parent knows, life is dearer for it; and in our case, after what we have been through as a family, the bond is indeed a genetic one. In the deepest terms there are it is creative.

'Somehow I am always in touch with a miracle,' I wrote when my younger son, sixteen years older than P., reached his third birthday. In India it was true in many ways. Jibanananda's freshness at the back of the maze was certainly one. But to have a daughter, in my case, is to have all the loveliness of Nature as a friend.

*W*hat is precious is how to keep the name
   of beauty in a place where you can find it.
It is in poetry and song and dance;
it's heard in someone speaking (in the someone
if not the speaking); in a red palash-*flower*
it breathes, and in a small goat nibbling it;
in things of sensible and fine design
it's found, a chair, a shoe; or a birthday-card
designed in loving humour (but not bought);
it's in a cool breeze when it's been too hot;
it's in light's everywhere, it's in night's silence.
And most of all it hides in happiness
of others. Beauty's name is all about you,
this day of days, when you are ten years old.

30

India is a careless land. Brute suffering is passed by. The travails of my family were little enough; and what there was to endure, we endured together to an extent. In any case it was quickly in the past. But everywhere, under every stone it seems, is a story to chill the blood. Stories of the underclass, rarely reported.

Anjali, like many village girls, was married very early. Abandoned by her husband she brought up her infant daughter, Rina, by working as a maid-servant in Calcutta, but couldn't educate her. When Rina was seventeen she was married to Narayan who lived with his widowed mother Parul in a village next to the one Anjali came from. As always the groom did not move and the bride lived with him in his parents' house. From the start Parul and Narayan put pressure on Rina to bring money from her mother. She refused. They insisted they were owed it as the dowry had been too small. Narayan gave up his job and the pressure increased. Rina did not give in. Husband and mother-in-law now gave bride a daily beating. Dowry harassment is common; they were able to

do it with impunity. Finally after four months of marriage
Narayan beat her with a stick, complaining of finding
insects in the food, and Parul contributed some sarcastic
comments. Something snapped in Rina and she tried to
leave the house. Her mother-in-law stopped her and later
in the day poured kerosene over her and set her ablaze. At
the time of the murder Narayan may have been out and
not a direct party to it. While Rina was on fire a relative
of Parul's, suspected himself of killing his daughter-in-
law, discouraged neighbours from coming to Rina's aid,
warning of problems with the police. Eventually Rina's
maternal uncles arrived from the next village and took her
to the local hospital with 80% burns. Anjali was informed.
Her employer's grown daughter came with her and they
collected Rina from the hospital and took her to one in
Calcutta with a burns unit. They were told there was no
bed available and at last she was put in an emergency ward
of a medical college, and given little attention, as often
happens with poor patients. She wanted to make a dying
declaration but no doctor would volunteer to take it down.
Someone from a women's organisation in Calcutta heard
about the case and at her insistence the declaration was
heard and recorded by the Calcutta police. Rina was in her
full senses when she made it and spoke in detail. She died
a few days later in the ward. Her maternal uncles recorded
the death in the police station of the village where she had
lived and the attack had taken place; but the police there
dragged their feet and Parul was not arrested. Pressure was
put on Anjali by neighbours and relatives on both sides
of the family to take 'mutual'. The word, adopted direct
into informal Bengali for such situations, means monetary

compensation on the condition of dropping charges. Rina's absentee father turned up and urged Anjali to agree, clearly after a share of the 'mutual' himself. Anjali refused. No arrest was made. The police delayed the proceedings till Parul and Narayan had escaped. It seemed they were bribed. They had not suggested the 'mutual' but indicated it as the way forward. The lady who told me all this had visited Rina where she lay in the ward and heard her story from her own, still living lips.

She was from the women's organisation and also saw Anjali and others involved. Nothing could be done. It was a not unusual case. According to the national crime record bureau there is a 'dowry death' in India every sixty-seven minutes. Dowry payment is illegal in India and practised almost as widely as ever. Even highly-educated and in other respects forward-looking families often still expect it, though in gifts more than in cash these days. A payment from the bride's family to the groom's, it hangs over a girl baby's head from the moment she is born, a black cloud, the sun over a boy's. For a villager it's a massive cash payment, often the equivalent of many years' earnings. With this vicious expectation added to that of a bride's servitude in the groom's parents' house, where he continues to live as a pampered child, the stage is set for the worst instincts to take over, greed, sadism, jealousy, contempt. Of course it does not happen in the vast majority of cases, and the payment often is token these days or waived altogether; but as the statistic shows the custom is a deadly blot on the scroll of citizenship.

Not that such an object exists: but in a day-to-day sense the invisible document lacks the robustness of a shared article of faith. The disfigurement has soaked through too deeply. Not the curse of dowry alone, but corruption in virtually all positions of public trust, caste prejudice, and ultimately the gap between rich and poor, currently increasing, saps the bond that makes strangers brothers. The cultural cloth of such fineness and firmness in the hinterland of the mind, the gods, the festivals, the participation in changing patterns of Time and Nature, the family duties, the recognition of the old, the tolerance of the young, none of this translates into something desperately needed in the foreground, nor can it. A touch of land-wide civic responsibility, trumpeted by politicians and newspaper editorials, is not there to be felt: there are too many entrenched interests. To go at it too hard distorts into a narrow nationalism. The ordinary Indian waits and hopes; and for now the suffering is passed by.

Another example: in Orissa (to the south of West Bengal) an Australian missionary is burnt to death in his car along with his two small sons. It's a reaction against the perceived threat of Hindus losing their identity to become Christian. (There's more of the same going on there as I write.) The numbers of converts are ridiculously small and freedom of religion is enshrined in the Constitution; but a fanatic movement has its way. There are two horrors: the last minutes of a good man and of two children; and the reaction of the central government. It is unconscionably slow in setting up an investigation. At one point it's a matter of finding an office from which to conduct it, that holds it up for months. One can see why. It's a matter of votes. Other examples are endless.

Political parties feed on this carelessness. They rush to

fill the vacuum in the public mind. Under an appearance of public-spiritedness they seize power over small communities. At election time suddenly it is no holds barred. The Communist Party that has been in power in West Bengal for a generation has perfected the art. It's left to the cadres to cast nets of dependency and fear while ministers profess ignorance; but everyone knows what's happening. The Party is extraordinarily far-reaching and well backed-up. And of course the ideal behind it has a deep hold in hearts and minds. If it would transmute, if it could transmute into a vehicle of respect for the individual, and of opportunity for ordinary people to work and care for their own, it would gain all the votes it needed and gain them honestly. And a movement might begin in the state of a true citizenship, to spread further afield. But it is feral.

*D*ried claws hooked in the ground: not trees,
    not life: then what iron nails are these?
What agent of death here chokes the land?
Free speech, free thought, free action's banned.
It has a thousand heads: and smiles,
its young men sing and march for miles –
but speak against it, worse still, threaten
to oust by vote: those faces deaden.
How does it send its messages?
Murder and rape in the villages,
shootings in a Calcutta lane.
Goddess of India – O Rain –
wash this demon from West Bengal!
Let openness flower – or else lose all.

31

There is a violence of old, in the ancient legends of India, that is essentially unheroic. The individual is not ennobled; and in terms of his responsibility to the need of others, to the demand of their inner freedom, it is a patchy story. An imbalanced equation is left. The reverence up and down the land for the Mahabharata and the Ramayana, after all this time, still is uncritical and in consequence these great epics, with their hold on the Indian imagination, delay the emergence of something like a constructive core to the community. Instead the swirling dark landscape of the poems takes its place in the roof of the mind, for all the multitudinous moments of splendour, as a luminous twilight, a day that cannot rise. Literature has been used in the West to seek out and re-define a redemptive quality: the individual battles through and though he may lose his life, comes clear. Some would say the Indian model is a truer one: he does not battle through but battles on. The instinctive journey however that literature undertakes towards a state of mind and a state of feeling, that is of the crucially refreshed persona

– in the end, a journey to enlightenment – is common. It is no doubt a part of the evolutionary effort. In the Mahabharata and the Ramayana one sees it at work. And one sees it falter in the ending.

In the Ramayana, the story of the man-god Ram, the hero's wife Sita is abducted by the demon Ravana. With the help of Hanuman, his trusted monkey follower, Ram rescues her. When Hanuman offers to put Sita's harsh wardresses to death she shows them a concern that strikes a rare and beautiful note: it is not their fault, and it is the part of noble people to show compassion to all. She looks forward to being reunited with her husband. But he acts strangely, has no warmth for her at all, and it comes out that he is convinced she has given in to Ravana's desires. There is no question of rape, only of her loyalty to Ram. She is shocked and vows to burn herself to death. A fire is kindled. Ram does nothing to prevent her stepping into it. The God of Fire rises out of the flames to gather up Sita and present her to Ram, unharmed; who accepts her and her innocence, saying her ordeal was to satisfy the public, and that he only appeared to doubt her. And so the story ends happily.

It is an example of something in evidence not only in old Indian stories but everywhere one turns. A woman is held up as possessed of virtue and treated like dirt. Apart from the ending the Ramayana is a delightful ramble through a forest of light and shade: the opulent display of Nature, a simplicity of spirit, spells, treachery, devotion, a rich pastoral. It is a kind of hymn to Mother Earth and to humans' place on it. The might of power, the tenderness of love, the thrill of sheer adventure carry one through to a callous end. The narrowly moralistic correctness of the Brahmin male, that will have been responsible for the homiletic element, is even now in place to be so, across the land as a whole. For the Brahmins are the priestly caste and cannot but admit a conservative element into what they stand for that is wildly anachronistic. The continuance of their claim by right to be sole priests has its own stultifying effect on the forward social thinking of what is in effect a Hindu nation.

The Mahabharata is *sui generis*. Thematically it is of war, family rivalry, human error, godly qualities, a vast tapestry that leads from episode to episode and finally seems to have reflected something of the journey of existence itself. And not merely the existence of one life, or one family, or one race; but of the charge that is carried by human time. Its sweep is violent and extraordinary. At the same time it is both almost criminally drawn-out and repetitive, and its value system, as in the social imperatives it presents, again and again quite simply is shocking. There can be no synopsis of a few lines but at the end the main family group, a group of five brothers and the wife they share, ascend a mountain with a dog that attaches itself to the eldest brother, Yudhisthira. (As with much else one that is unusual to the modern eye, one takes the marital arrangement in one's stride – one is a little uncomfortable with it perhaps, but lets it pass.) Yudhisthira has been directly responsible for the most appalling and prolonged suffering on the part of the family, gambling away his kingdom and wife Draupadi – who is restored to them after hideous shame – in a dice game. Finally the kingdom is re-won and after a time of peace the eldest brother decides to renounce the world. The five and Draupadi dress in tree-bark and start to climb the great mountain Meru.

First Draupadi collapses on the slope. One of the brothers, Bhima, a gentle giant in peace and fearsome in battle, asks Yudhisthira why she has fallen. She was over-partial to one of her husbands, comes the reply. She is left where she lies. A younger brother, Sahadeva, can go no further. Bhima asks: he was always humble, why has he fallen? Too proud of his sagacity, says Yudhisthira, and he is abandoned too. The next to come to a standstill is Sahadeva's twin, Nakula. Yudhisthira tells Bhima he was too conscious of his good looks. Arjuna, the fabulously gifted brother with a touch of the divine, goes down. A great archer but contemptuous of other archers, explains the eldest. Bhima himself falls. You were a selfish eater, says Yudhisthira, and leaves him too in his wake. So the survivor climbs, dog following, and is met by Indra, the king of the gods. Indra says Draupadi and the others have left their bodies and attained heaven, where Yudhisthira may now go bodily to meet them. But leave the dog behind, says Indra. Yudhisthira is shocked at this and says he can't leave the loyal dog behind. At which the dog reveals himself to be a god, Yudhisthira is congratulated on his noble behaviour and taken heavenward.

He successfully undergoes another test of character, volunteering to stay where his presence lends comfort to the tortured souls of his brothers and wife who appear to be in a kind of Purgatory, rather than proceed on his own to heaven. And with that he sees his brothers and his wife among the gods, the illusion of their suffering is dispelled, and the epic at last ends with the celestial state bestowed upon them all.

Yes, I am not Indian and I do not see things the Indian way. Yes, even I can see something twistedly true in the relentless bowing to events. But the redemptive sequence of the final passage is formulaic not felt. And the high-handedness of the major character is dumbfounding.

And no-one in India will whisper it.

It is discourteous of me to make these judgements. I hope that the right to criticise and be criticised (in what is after all a democracy) will alleviate the offence. There is much in the ancient texts of India of piercing insight and wisdom. The psychological awareness reflected in the Upanishads is ennobling, one feels, for all time. The Ramayana and the Mahabharata contain a great deal that for the best reasons will never die. But the ground of India is too dry, too dry. My half-baked notions are merely there to be swept aside by Mahakala, by Time's great force. I cannot ask forgiveness, but for the reader's indulgence, that they form and the account lets them appear.

Thousands of years, like atoms of dust, are lost,
   spun out in space; the present is all there is;
an uncomprehending ground that swelters beneath
an invisible choking mist of memories.
Confused, bruised dreams: some words of forest-leaf
long since crushed and crumbled in scholars' sand;
an ingrained knowledge of weariness and death;
a fury-account that cannot count the cost;
a custom of cruelty beyond belief ...
what should I do in this cracked, heat-driven land?
Thousands of years will merely whirl away;
and yet I set my foot down here for later.
Somewhere I see a huge yellow butterfly play;
and endless paddy-fields, knee-deep in water.

32

In economic terms the inertia of India is less apparent. Calcutta is on the move. Not as swiftly as Delhi or Mumbai; but even this recalcitrant old city is starting to bust out of its chrysalis. It will take a while. The trickle-down effect of capital to the worst-off that is reduced to the slowest of drips in the villages is scarcely more lenient to the urban poor. As the middle class grows and grows richer the underclass grows and barely subsists. The gap is wider than ever. That there are social dangers in this hardly needs saying. The vacuum is not likely to succumb either to home-brewed revolution or to a whirlwind religious mania driving south. India is a tolerant place. But while the rewards of globalisation, if it can be managed, are stupendous, and as all-reaching as the term implies, the perils are real. A platitude, but one feels it, dimly, living in Calcutta.

Or Kolkata as I really should call it, looking at the present, and the future in the present. Again I apologise to Kolkatans for being lodged half in the past. I want to show the modern city. The new name is a butterfly, beating independently in the air, not perched and waiting to take off like the old one. Yet for me and my account the old one still is the more apposite. There was a glorious moment in the Calcutta International School Society, as the school I taught at termed itself on its books and so on, when the city's change of name came into being. A host of exercise-books sported a new acronym. But like the Calcutta Club and other well-established institutions the school stayed with the older name. The enthusiasm of the boys and girls was cut short.

The school offers a poignant image of the needs of development. First a massive new shopping mall reared its head to the sky right next to it. Then the school was razed to the ground as the mall needed a car-park. In fairness the school was too small and had been intending to relocate for a time; and it became a smarter and bigger institution further from the city centre. P. finished her schooldays in the small old building where the staffroom tripled as library and extra classroom: her cohort, the last to do so, seem to share a pang of outrage at the past turned to flat tarmac. A totalitarian authority (a covert impulse of the laissez-faire new world?) has re-cast the watering-hole of their childhood. Their stamping-ground as social animals has been airbrushed out. Or so it can seem; though of course they know it is not as sinister as that, and that the change must be. The new school is applauded but something of the old loveliness is snatched away.

I worked there as the new mall went up and even after years of seeing it round the city, could not get used to the balancing act on bamboo poles used as scaffolding. I was told by the school canteen stall owner, who operated more or less directly beneath, that a workman had fallen from them to his death. It was in the holidays, one would say fortunately for the schoolchildren, were it not for the blind horror. It is all too easy to see the promise of a fair future as a false god demanding sacrifice. But in effect it is nothing new; the world does improve; and globalisation, so far from being a new phenomenon, has been on the march from day one.

The city is looking up in so many ways. When I arrived in '94 it took seven years to get a telephone. When I left a dozen years on it took three weeks. Now mobile phones are beginning to swarm. I must interject an early memory of my stay. I was wandering in a relatively poor area in the city's north and stopped for a glass of tea at a stall. The owner, squatting bare-chested on the counter, insisted on preparing a special infusion for which he charged an extra rupee. He went through the prestidigitatory art of straining the liquid through muslin and pouring from container to container with great aplomb, finally handing it to me with a flourish – and a 'phone rang loudly. I had no idea where it could be. He grunted and plucked a mobile from behind a saucepan and answered it. I sipped in appreciation.

A far cry from his counterpart on the outskirts of a village whom I occasionally passed on my way in. A tall, bespectacled, thinly-clad old man, he too squatted all day on his stall counter, but not in the here-and-now of mobile calls. He read the Bhagavad Gita over and over. It is perhaps the holiest text, a part of the Mahabharata, on the surface a discussion of when duty calls to war, in essence an awakening of the burning conscience of the individual.

The old gentleman would sit or squat for ever it seemed, reading the old Sanskrit, meditating, and occasionally, with a certain fine deliberation, pouring tea.

The two keep their stalls at opposite corners in a collage in my mind. City and country much is happening and not happening. In Calcutta smart grocer's wares squeeze their prepackaged way into tiny shops. Marks and Spencer may be about to invade. 'Next' flags up a clothes outlet. Air-conditioned shopping malls rise from nowhere. Coffee shops burgeon; a café culture dots the streets. Apartment complexes rise: young men are beginning to set up for themselves, and to take their brides somewhere where they can be at home without the immediate weight of expectation of in-laws. The Metro is extending from a single straight line to a wider arterial system. Private hospitals are being started up by Indian doctors coming in from abroad who see a good business opportunity with the expanding middle class. For by and large it is all a middle-class bonanza. The Indian industrial giant firm of Tata is working on a relatively cheap car, the Nano, to cater to them. Yet it is still the same old Calcutta.

Maybe a few more of the girl-children of the poor are going to school. It is not certain and no-one is very concerned. Slums are cleared and relocate themselves. Groups still sleep, cook, make love, give birth and die on the streets. Some Muslim areas especially stay undeveloped and may be getting worse. A charitable organisation has set up some public toilets in the city; the two main stations are smarter than they were; battered buses are replaced (to stay as crowded as before). But Calcutta is still a massive village of hand-to-mouth subsistence for the majority;

with the faint outline of a modern metropolis for a few. Despite the international brands for the rich in the new malls, corruption clogs the engine; the outline will lag behind its definition. Inertia adds its deadly drop of poison. In villages and small towns of West Bengal there are improvements but the rate of progress, by and large, is bleaker still.

But this is economic progress, not happiness. I like to think of a certain crossroads near the heart of Calcutta, that harbours an arts complex, as emblematic for the whole of the state, indeed for the country. In a light way Rabindra Sadan embodies Tagore's dictum for India: to offer the best of her culture and to accept from others their best. Theatres, a cinema, a gallery, a hall, a stage for cultural events, a lake: the place is enchanted. It rests the soul. Couples and single people find their ease near the white buildings. Sometimes in the evening a bearded fellow wanders about singing Tagore songs. It is a gift to be there.

*F*ountains and freewheeling birds in an evening performance
   upstage the American film. A boy selling tea
stars in an instant's unrehearsed role. The arms
of the dusk-trees, extravagant directors,
bring on the night. Unprompted a queue moves on.
Outside the Academy of Fine Arts a series
of souls is on show. A textiles exhibition
of saris and coloured shirts; a chiselled carving
again and again, of the human form at ease;
a portrait, suddenly, of a Calcuttan face
at night. I am in a gleaming world-city's
late festival. What poems are here, what songs,
what leaf-notes, in a sparkle of conversation,
under the spotlight of a quarter-moon.

33

Sealdah Station at dawn is a powerhouse. Sealdah means jackal-place, intriguingly for the city's maintown terminus, and the suggestion of a feral pack going about its business lingers somehow in the swarming restlessness that pervades it. Vast queues at the ticket counters, newspaper vendors slapping down their wares about the forecourt, commuters dodging one another, massing at the platforms. Antisocials, as they are termed, turn up here and there, beggars, mad people: these days there are fewer of them, the place is smarter than it was, but still a naked man may suddenly appear, 'out of it', and a criminal element is never absent. The homeless now do not sleep on the platforms as they used to, more order is creeping in, but the tide of travellers, vendors of various kinds, loiterers, and crammed, untidy trains still has an untamed charge. An urban station is the same anywhere, to a degree, but Calcutta is not 'respectable' yet, nor are its main termini, Sealdah and Howrah. Day and night the 'jackal station' is alert with an impulse, the raw nerve of the city.

Local trains take two million passengers a day in and out. The journeys can be an endurance test but it is partly what you are used to. A few times I witnessed a degradation of the human animal that made the most crowded, stifling and insect-ridden journey seem like nothing. The first time something bumped my leg under the seat. A small boy crawled through and out into the aisle, utterly blackened and filthy, a dustpan in his hand. He looked up at those standing round him and tapped those seated on the knee, asking for small change. Then under the seats again. It is like sending boys up chimneys, possibly worse. One hardly likes to think of the vicious control of his takings, and his life, there may have been in the background. Sometimes one sees a scuttling boy in a comparatively uncrowded train but when it is at its worst it is all too vivid, an image of hell.

More and more voices are raised these days against child labour and yet I have seen many examples of it in India working well, so to speak. One such case was at a friend's house in a village where a ten-year-old girl was playing with the two young daughters of the couple and over the evening helped with a few domestic duties before going to bed. I asked my friend's wife about her. "She works here." A large family in the village had asked for her to be taken on. She was not attending school, but neither would she had she stayed with her own family. As it was she picked up a good deal from the new household (including the basics of chess from me over a half-hour session – we could not speak much but she was quick). When I visited again in a couple of years she was gone; her family had withdrawn her 'to be married'. Again, one has seen boys serving at tables in restaurants who pick up a little English and other languages from tourists, and have a secure home sleeping on the floor and roughly cared for by the management, far better off than they may have been otherwise. But endless horrors on the other side, small children dying slowly in brick factories to name just one, make it an argument with no easy answers at present. It is usually an academic discussion anyway, in that a capability is assumed on the country's part of ensuring the law is observed, or of oversight of conditions, that is not much more than wishful thinking. Slowly, what is broadly acceptable changes for the good, market forces change it for the bad, and the cover-up goes on.

At a large metropolitan station however everything is uncovered in a sense. The endless procession of trains announces somehow the working of the body of the land, that it is so much a part of. The circulation of the system is felt, and a brute warmth that is taken for granted, and in spite of the downside and because of it as well, a nameless reassurance.

But a moment of brutality can send the system into shock. In the first year of my stay a political earthquake hit the station with tremors across the state. Mr Chakraborty, a college lecturer travelling with some students, was held at Sealdah for not being able to present a ticket. His students complained that he was treated with discourtesy and incited a crowd against the station officials who called in the police. The crowd was further incensed at this and threw bricks. A policeman's cheek was torn. The mob was finally dispersed by the police firing at it. Six were killed.

Every college and school in the state shut down the next

day in sympathy with the victims of the police. Every newspaper made the same noise. The minister responsible for the police (who was to become the Chief Minister of West Bengal) either then or later said he was unable to control them. It didn't seem possible to criticise Mr Chakraborty, the students or the brick-throwers however mildly. The spasm ceased as abruptly as it started, a new atrocity no doubt now centre page.

Clearly the police were very much at fault. A number of them, probably under-trained, panicked and acted unforgivably. It was the lack of any kind of a balanced discussion that was disturbing in the aftermath. At the same time there were riots on the streets of the southern city of Bangalore. It was a language issue: the minority tongue was allowed so much air-wave time within certain hours of the day. The news was read in it at the wrong time. Twenty-eight were killed.

The nerve of violence in the land is the real issue. The philosophical systems that have originated there, including Buddhism, have done more than all others to quell the human tendency to run amok. The importance of comparatively recent thinkers such as Ramakrishna, of whom more later, and Tagore, is that they continue the Indian tradition of a true contribution. The elements of violence are not static and the powers to combat them continually form also. To a small but real extent the country is the crucible for the melting of the metals. The answer is ongoing as is the problem.

One of my many excursions from Sealdah was to a small town in the north of the state. There was a poetry conference of some kind; but I fell out with the organisers before it began. They met me at the station and took me to a hotel room and then would not leave me alone. I had had a long sleepless journey and after an hour or two of snacks and courtesies I asked to be left to rest. They wouldn't hear of it. It was time to eat. I realised I was in for it. I was actually quite ill with tiredness and said I really had to rest. Quite a pretty conversation ensued. We have a duty as your hosts. But can't you see that I'm not well? Then you must eat. But I've been eating. You must eat properly. If you have a duty as my hosts, don't you have a duty to my feelings? We have a duty to your stomach. At which immortal line I lost my temper and threw them out of the room and was reviled the following evening at the conference, no doubt quite rightly.

But what I remember with more relish is the table-tennis the next morning at a youth club that I stumbled upon nearby, and at which I was made royally welcome. The instructor was about my age, we were evenly matched, and the boys made a gladiatorial event of it. And often I am back walking the roads of the town in the afternoon, and pausing in an ordinary street for ever, and for no reason at all seeing Jibanananda Das in my mind, and writing a poem for him, or he for me.

*W*ashing-line shadows shape a face on the grass
    that's snatched away; two new-hacked piles of logs
at once are dead and living; a mint spins out gold coins
down a still line of marigold-terrace-pots;
the rickshaw-bicycle-birds hoot, squeal and scream
over a still path of the sky – the road
that does not change.

                  All is a smalltown moment
in West Bengal.

            A gasp of pain's in the air;
Jibanananda is standing in the road;
his eyes see through the ashen manuscripts
his hand must still compile – must still compile –
bare lonely hand – now with thud after thud
an axe cleaves through a log – and my breath shudders
as a pen's line records a gasp of beauty.

34

Visited by a poet then, as I stood looking at the day's eternal traffic, in the idle place of the mind, I see a different figure now. He was a soldier-politician hunted by the British for good reason in the Second World War, as he travelled to Soviet Russia (in the aftermath of the Nazi-Soviet Pact), Germany and Japan, for support to harry the colonial power in India and win independence for his country. On the principle that my enemy's enemy is my friend he sought to undermine Britain at all costs, and managed to raise a force in Japan of liberated Indian prisoners of war, the Indian National Army. But a foray into India failed in its main intent, to attract large-scale desertion from the Indian Army (that was engaged under British command against the Japanese); and in practical military terms the movement was short-term and unsuccessful. Yet he was one of the greatest unifiers of men the nation has seen.

Subhas Chandra Bose, who came to be known simply as Netaji (literally Respected Leader), was a Bengali born in Orissa in 1897 and educated at Cambridge University.

Quickly involving himself in Calcuttan politics, he was imprisoned for organising a boycott of the celebrations to mark the visit of the Prince of Wales to India in 1921. In jail again on suspicion of terrorism, and again for leading an 'Independence Procession' protesting against British Rule, on his third release he was elected Mayor of Calcutta in 1930. Several more short terms of imprisonment followed. The British exiled him to Europe where he continued to campaign for Independence. He married his German secretary in 1937 and they had a daughter. Here the story ran into trouble with his admirers many years later, long after he had disappeared from the horizon. In the early 'nineties a distribution van for a Calcuttan daily newspaper was hijacked and thousands of copies of the paper burnt. It carried a report of love-letters between the couple.

It had been thought he was chaste and unmarried and the discovery that he was not as a pure *sannyasi* (holy man) could not be borne. The news had to be a lie. But it was accepted soon enough. Netaji made no known claim to be chaste or holy: it was a superimposed quality of the kind the Indian public loves to claim in its heroes. A spurious grace attaches itself to a larger-than-life figure who comes to symbolise an inner greatness of the Indian spirit. The idea of the meditative recluse, the sage of the past, may have led in some part to the premium set on chastity, though there are plenty of stories of sages with wives. The figure of Netaji continues to be viewed with a reverence that verges on the irrational. He disappeared in 1945 but many of sound mind cherish a hope he is alive (at 111).

He began his public career as an acolyte of Gandhi but

split with him. "If people slap you once, slap them twice," was his answer to the doctrine of the other cheek. During the Second World War he did the rounds of Britain's enemies as described; and his most powerful words came in a rallying call to Indians in Burma, "Give me blood and I shall give you freedom!" Two slogans are his, Chalo Delhi! (On to Delhi!) and Jai Hind! (Victory to India!) The latter, taken up by the independent government later, is now like a thought of India itself, a breath in the national consciousness. In part it was his words that made him so beloved. But in greater part it was indeed the pure metal of the man. He was the only Hindu leader to have had the complete trust of Muslims, who were content to share with Hindus and others under his command, to eat with them and be one with them, for with him they were all Indians. He was incorruptible; he raised the flag high of an independent India, a fearless land that had its pride. Who knows what might have been, had he returned from hiding and military setback at Independence? But it was not to be. In 1945 a Tokyo-bound plane he was on was reported to have crashed over Taiwan. Amid rumours of sabotage he was declared dead.

A remarkable mystery now began. For there were further rumours that he had not been on the plane, or that there had been no crash: then where was Netaji? And for some still, where is Netaji? An enquiry in 1956 was inconclusive. In 2005 the Taiwan Government confirmed there had been no crash with him on board and none in that time-frame. People one meets now will argue the facts and theories for hours. My view is that he may have become a *sannyasi* (ironically enough) in Uttar Pradesh in the north. A mysterious Hindu monk named Bhagwanji lived there, dying (perhaps) in 1985; there is some telling evidence for the identification.

It is one of the great stories of the land. Bengalis have a deep affection for him and a sense of what-might-have-been. Though Attlee's government brought independence to India shortly after the war, the Churchillian disregard for the place and its people that emanated from the colonial power till 1945 had done little to encourage confidence. I was appalled when I first heard of Netaji's visits to Germany and Japan, and something in me still is; but I came to admire the man's vision and utter grit, even if he miscalculated. India is awash with extraordinary personalities. No doubt as every country, one way or another, it tends not to see its national figures clear.

It looks to them, perhaps, for something that is right in front of their eyes. In the small town to which I travelled for the poetry conference, and in which so much happened to me in two days, I met an elderly gentleman who invited me to his house for a cup of tea. I went and was introduced to his mother, a blind lady in white widow's weeds of nearly a hundred. As I came into the garden she was squatting on a step murmuring a prayer. Her son said it was a prayer for him; she had said one for him, as the eldest son, every day of his life. I asked if I might talk with her when she was ready and so I found myself sitting with her, holding her hand and exchanging trivial words that seemed to have great meaning. Hardly had we sat down however than the son was waving at me to come to where he was the other side of the garden. I pretended not to see and we talked a little more; then he appeared and insisted I come right away. I followed him to his study where, bursting with importance, he told me of his Ph.D. and showed me his thesis (on folk-song) and a newspaper clipping about the award and his future aims and heaven knows what else, till I had to go. I did not see his mother as I went. But to me she is India.

My attendance at the conference may not have been entirely disastrous; for a speech I made there was remembered in part by a young man who quoted some words to me years later when I ran into him by chance at the Calcutta Book Fair. I had said I was a poet, a guest in India, a guest in my own country, a guest of the world. The last phrase (*ami prithibir atithi*) he repeated with an urgent emphasis: he knew, he understood. A good moment.

But not as moving as that with the aged lady in the summerhouse, never to be forgotten. The old India and the new, if I am to be pessimistic, were in that garden. The old is everywhere, in people of all ages, and it is to them that the eye of the public must surely turn, to find greatness, that is its own greatness. But it is so in every land and very much in that to which I have returned. We bend to the light, to strain from the root at our peril.

*B*lind, perched on the step, she blesses her son.
Her silent lips, of near a century's breath,
call God to Earth, out-sing the dust of death,
whisper a prayer that lights on everyone
and one alone. Each day she blesses him.
In widow's white, like a frail lovely bird,
she waits to go.

         I hear the day's true word,
Mother of India, an awakening hymn
of love.

        But now the son has summoned me.
I get the lowdown on his Ph.D.,
the tome itself, with all the rest of it,
press-cuttings, even the letter of notification
(xeroxed). He too waits heaven's invitation:
'Perhaps, before I die, I'll be D.Litt.'

35

It was my privilege to know an ordinary person throughout my time in India who was as extraordinary as any. Soon after I appeared on a local television programme early on, I was sitting in a café trying to translate a poem when someone sat down opposite me and said he'd been keeping the waiters at bay who apparently had wanted to throw me out. I hadn't realised how long I'd been sitting there with coffee finished. He had recognised me from the programme and took it upon himself to let me get on with the work. This first act was typical. Subhasis saw beyond the person to the need.

Over the years we were to share innumerable café tables, restaurant meals, drinks, and not entirely in words, for one does not tell all, yet on the table between us so to speak, the story of our lives. He worked as the financial clerk in a small firm of Gujarati businessmen who nakedly exploited any of the workforce not of their own state. This is to be expected anywhere in India whatever the background of the management. In this case Subhasis, the lone Calcuttan in a firm in his own city, was put upon more than most.

His wage was minimal – about two thousand five hundred rupees a month when I first knew him. At that time my early retirement pension from teaching in the UK came out to fifteen times the amount. (I may add he only once asked me to lend some money, which I did.) He accepted the protectionist culture at work with a good grace but what went against the grain was the falsification of the accounts that he was regularly called upon to make. He had worked for the firm about fifteen years and it was his job to save them money at the hands of the taxman.

There is probably not a firm in the world that does not go in for a certain amount of bamboozlement in this matter and in Calcutta it is as automatic as breathing. There is no straight line in the financial world. As well as a skirting of the rocks at annual audit there are the inspectors of one kind or another who try to come on board: in India it's a dirty but open steering. Fairy-tales and hand-outs keep the boat afloat. Subhasis was a man of the world and saw it all with a wry amusement but at the same time hated what he did. But jobs are a torture to find in middle age. He had family commitments. Most of the time his day's work was a model of probity. He got on with the people, as he tended to do with all, and knew his personal contribution was valued. He continued.

One day he came round to talk looking aghast. After initially dismissing a tip-off from an acquaintance of his wife's infidelity he had discovered her with an old friend of the family in a tell-tale scenario. Over the next few years he managed to contain the situation: the friend was still his friend, and more than that to his wife, who depended on her husband's capacity to bear a burden at whatever cost, more than she knew. He realised it had started far back and refused to go into the implications of that. He had help from a psychiatrist for a time who said the patient anticipated the doctor's advice at every session. Still he needed to hear it. The situation limped along, the daughter of the family growing into her teens. Then out of the blue, a demand at work suddenly unacceptable, he threw in his job.

About four years followed of acute difficulty. He was disoriented to a degree, unable to find work except in unsatisfactory patches, haunted by the home situation, finding it difficult to fill in the time, always giving his wife space, never setting down the burden. He would not injure other people's feelings or dislodge the fragile nest of the household. Eventually he did find a proper job and one he was more suited to; and with his daughter taking her place at university, was able to settle into a semi-detached situation as regards the family and from a little distance, continue as carefully committed as ever. Meanwhile there had been almost a soap opera of family difficulties among the relatives that he had to deal with.

I met his father once, early on: though very weak, he talked humorously and left a certain impression of the endurability of all things, an indefinable oneness with life that seemed to be passed on. He had lit out on his own at an early age and lived with the consequences. Subhasis' mother died a few years after her husband; and his mother-in-law died at about the same time as the result of an accident: her clothes caught fire. His wife had more to deal with. Her younger sister acted strangely, marrying in haste and divorcing with more speed. Her mother and this sister had taken up the cause of stray dogs and cats with a kind of witless zeal, continually taking on more of them in an unhealthy living situation. In the middle of it all her brother committed suicide. These events were not in the order described but they happened all within a few years and Subhasis was forever dealing with what needed to be done. Nothing was too much. A small man with the shoulders of Atlas, he has helped me to bear a burden of the past. I have not spoken of it to him, but there is a level at which he will know it.

He was passionate about poetry. (He was after all a Calcuttan.) He wrote a fine elegy on his father's passing, that I translated, called 'Only the Chapter's End.' One verse went: 'Time after time I heard the harsh speech of anger; / and the silent motions of his eyes still deeply saw. / Hard-sorrowing, still he'd put a hand on my shoulder: / in the heart's song the generation gap was no more.' The poem ended: 'and pluck new morning from the stem of a dream.' It is one of those moments in words that say all that is needed and resist analysis. His most powerful poem I saw was written after a newspaper report of a vagrant who had hanged himself from a branch of a tree in the Maidan, the green strip at the heart of the city. The poem was called 'Pendulum' and it followed the dead eyes' view as the corpse slowly swung. The lines seemed to go from side to side with the body as one read. It was a vision that mixed life and death from a mind steeped in the overlap of the two, and rich in the knowledge of its land.

R. and I needed to find a larger flat, with a room for P. and space for three people to be together and apart. This was scarcely an Indian luxury but one I was used to and my pension, that went a long way in India (but goes nowhere in England), made it possible. We found a glorious place in Jodhpur Park, a little south of Ballygunge where I had lived a few months before Park Street. It was fourth floor, with a balcony (important to R. and later very much to me), five rooms including a massive one I could put my books all round, and stone floors with intriguing patterns. There was no lift but we took the necessary exercise as a plus. We moved in; and the first couple of weeks were sheer hell, the landlord (who lived elsewhere) suddenly taking fright, it appeared, at our unmarried status and turning legalistic to an insane degree. Finally it was all sorted out and we were able to breathe again.

I have fallen in love with a suite of rooms,
  and made my proposal, and been accepted.
I am the happiest of bridegrooms:
if ever man made a vow and kept it,
it is my word. A sweetness blooms
in our first days, so passionate-hectic:
what storm's surliness could affect it?
But the bride's father fearfully looms.

It's a kind of cold war – how the money is paid –
instructions rescinded – the climate is Arctic –
the law triple-checking each syllable said:
a deadly manoeuvring is the trade-tactic.
Hit on the head by an iron bar,
what terms can I reach with my father-in-law?

36

The family settled in Jodhpur Park. R. set up a new NGO that worked specifically with women and children, mainly in villages in Darjeeling District but also in Purulia District and in the city. Its base was the new flat.

It was named DANA, which means wing or wings in Bengali, and doubled as an English acronym for the official title, Development & Awareness Need Art. It is not uncommon for an NGO to have an English title; the one R. had founded with her father many years before was Centre for Communication and Cultural Action (CCCA). It had worked mainly in rural communities through the use of folk media and particularly theatre to raise consciousness and open a path to personal and social development. R. had started a branch for women called Muktadhara (Free Current, and the title of a play by Tagore) to give women of the depressed section their own voice. Except for certain reserved rituals and scorned professions they are crowded out of the performance arts and relegated to the background in constructional ones such as pottery. DANA was to add wings to the intent of the previous venture. With women and children at the heart of the new organisation R. was able to initiate an active and outward-looking mode of operation that was something quite new in development work, and gave many women a wider horizon (literally), and their communities a way to see them with fresh eyes.

I loathe the language I have used in the last sentence. It comes in part from my having spent some time helping with DANA's official applications for a grant. But the pi tone is more or less inescapable. And it could not be further removed from R.'s approach. More than anyone I have known she enters the world of those she talks with, leaving her own behind. In fact her background is not so different from a village-woman's. While most townspeople inhabit a different planet, for all their concern, R. spent several years as a young married woman in a village at the service of her husband's household. But she is the kind of person, rarest of all, whose mind and heart are at the service of whoever she speaks with.

Poetry, song, painting, puppetry, dance, ceramics, theatre of many kinds, all are used by DANA to get to grips with the straitjacket village society slips its women into from birth. Its policy is to involve men as well as women. It is a magnificent idea, to use local forms of art to explore issues, possibilities, a new way of thinking, and in its few years of existence DANA has had some real success. (Since R.'s coming to England its work has continued under the leadership of the committee and she has returned to India for a time to assist.) Its most memorable activity has probably been the *chetana-chala* or Awareness Journey.

There have been three of these. In the first some twenty-five women and seven men travelled from the hills of Darjeeling District to visit four villages in the plains in Purulia. They were Lepchas, one of the oldest tribes of India, now fast losing its identity in the overlapping currents of Buddhism and Christianity and Hindu life. They worship the mountain Kanchenjunga and a woman has real standing in their midst. Nevertheless in economic matters she is still restrained. These individuals had not been out of the hills and to meet women of the plains, in the more repressive culture of Purulia District, and to share ideas and experience through theatre and artistic workshops and performance and discussion forums, was the entire point. They also visited Calcutta. Later about twenty-five Purulian woman journeyed to villages in the same District to put on a programme of dance and drama arising from the festival of *karam* (a kind of tree). This is an ancient recognition of Nature's blessing, of the sort that has essentially vanished from Western life, and is alive all over India. In the old times young unmarried girls used to look after the seed for the crops and it was held that if the seed was good not only would the village prosper but the girls would be married that year. Still, fifteen days before the festival, village girls collect soil from the riverside, store it in a bowl and sow five sorts of seed in it, with a branch of the *karam*-tree planted in the bowl. For two weeks the seeds are watched over by the girls with ritual song and dance (as well as by the branch). Finally on *karam* day the girls roam here and there with the bowl, free from household duties, and also free to give vent to opinions they would normally not dare to whisper. With DANA

married and unmarried women alike put on a dramatic
performance using *karam* songs and called *mayeder galpo
meyeder galpo*, Stories of Mothers, Stories of Daughters.
Acted and sung in villages that already knew of the
festival, it will surely have sown a seed in many lives. The
third *chetana-chala* (a term I thought up and was delighted
to find fit for use and adopted) was a return visit by
fifteen Purulian women and two men to Lepcha villages,
the people of the plains for the first time ascending the
hills. Workshops and performance again touched a nerve,
directly addressing the question of women's rights, and
opened horizons.

In her workshops R. has with others composed songs
that are known and loved by hundreds of thousands of
village-women. 'If our eyes don't see it, If our ears don't
hear it, If our eyes don't see it, If our ears don't hear it, O
band of women, How long will it be, In the silence all of us
will suffer endlessly.' The beginning two lines are magical
in the Bengali, *dekte na pai chokhe, sunte na pai kane* ... and
the melody is mysterious, melancholic and joyful in one.
'Hang behind and linger, It is to stay under, Hang behind
and linger, It is to stay under, O band of women, How
long will it be, In the silence all of us will suffer endlessly.'
And the final verse, 'There's still time to say it, Shout it
out and cry it, There's still time to say it, Shout it out and
cry it, Come one and all, Say it with a will, Tell the world
there is no need to bear the sadness still.' R. has written
many poems, less lyrical and more subtle than her songs,
and often touching more or less directly on the story of
women, of mothers and daughters. She is someone with a
wholly practical sense of things who has poetry at her core.

In the new flat in Jodhpur Park DANA was started and from there it flourished. Its rationale, finally, is to make no distinction between the practical and the artistic; to follow the view that within the living soul of a community, the two are one. Its founder is someone who has made a difference.

'The soil in which we are born is the soil of our village,' said Tagore. India is its villages: every country is its villages, but beneath the polished surface of an urban economy, the treasure of our inheritance is shipwrecked and lost. As a parallel institution to the school and university in Santiniketan, and in a neighbouring village, Tagore founded a rural reconstruction centre, Sriniketan (Abode of Wellbeing). He was the first to conduct experiments in rural community development, setting up inter-cooperative banks and sending his son to Illinois to study agricultural science, to pass on the knowledge gained. The centre is still going. I went to a fair in the village of Sriniketan one January; a modest affair, at which I felt a great ease. The treasure of our inheritance is its simplicity, something that Tagore knew, that R. knows, that I have begun to learn.

*L*ight musical
tunes of sunlight:
cheap town goods, and
village craftsmen
burnishing, carving;
children hurrying;
colours of movement;
games of chance and
try-your-luck skill;
under a tree's arms,
in a wide orbit,
a turning freedom
of the world's fresh
afternoon.

37

P. grew up in the new home. After the initial difficulty with the management of Calcutta International School she entered a class of twenty-five or so that was vivid with character. I taught it myself, for no more than a lesson a week, in her second year there and retain an impression of one of the more interesting tangles of personality I've had the privilege of engaging with. I'm reminded of a delightful incident in my younger son's infancy. Many years back I and my earlier family in England were visiting relatives in the countryside and at two years old he was much taken with the cats and dogs that abounded in the large farmhouse. There was an armchair in the sitting-room that drew his attention and he manfully climbed over the arm and dropped into it, onto a snoozing ball of four or five kittens that shot off on his arrival in different directions like erratic particles in a CERN accelerator. For five minutes or so he stood in the chair, possessed and jabbering, articulating his excitement in a blaze of lucidity, no-one around able to understand a syllable. It stays as a minor highlight, so to speak, in the family memory scrapbook. I'd like to think I got further with 9B than he did with the kittens though to some, I'm sure, my efforts to teach poetry were equally incomprehensible. At any rate I enjoyed the encounter.

P.'s previous school had been English-medium and by the time she went to Calcutta International School, at 13, she was equally at ease in English and Bengali. Partly through my influence she had begun an engagement with English literature that was clearly to last for life. She loved Shakespeare and over her teens we read many of his plays together, and all the sonnets, as well as a fair sprinkling of other authors. I would have been glad if she could have kept up an early interest in Bengali poetry too; but while she would occasionally take up a translation of mine she found the originals hard going and seemed to come to a decision in her teens, to give herself breathing-space to enjoy literature with all her being. The English canon was the way.

How could one not be delighted, as a teacher and poet? My children have inherited my interest in literature counter-intuitively, my two sons finding poetry a closed book and my step-daughter naturally at home in its pages. In fact my contribution has been a consolidatory one, for when I met P. she reeled off a poem by Tagore called 'Birpurush', or 'Hero'. In eight eight-line stanzas a small boy tells of a journey with his mother. She is being carried like an aristocratic lady in a palanquin and he is riding like a prince at her side. They find a mysterious beautiful lake in a deserted area. Suddenly dacoits (highwaymen) approach. The palanquin-bearers hide. Khoka, the boy, saves the day, triumphant in a ferocious fight, and his mother breathes her relief he was there. In the poem he is reminding her of the events as they happened, including what they said to each other; while underneath, finely unsaid, both know it is all his imagination. P. had learnt the whole thing returning to it evening after evening with her mother, and I could hardly believe the clarity and expressiveness the six-year-old gave to her rendering. The memory feat was remarkable in itself and how she said it was more so: and I have never heard her say a Bengali poem again. That little mite, eyes on fire, has stayed in my mind as I have helped the person she became to explore the great English writers. It is the way life goes, and overall and not merely with regard to literature it has gone a way that calls unequivocally for celebration. Now at university in England studying Drama and English the little mite goes from strength to strength. The nourishment she takes is still that of her Bengali cradle. And, marvellously, she is a citizen of the world and at home in more than one local medium.

It is not mere self-indulgence that prompts me to tell some part of her linguistic story. It is a way in, if from an unusual angle, to a complex business, the role of English in India. It is one of the two official national languages, the other, Hindi, finding no more than a partial acceptance in the South. Hindi might have been imposed at Independence as the sole main tongue but local jealousies ran high and for many good reasons it was not done. (Though as I write I wonder what Netaji may have brought as a unifying leader to the post-war situation, including to the impending fault-line of Partition.) English, it is now clear, is the lingua franca of the globe, it is becoming everyone's second or third language. As a de-politicised colonising agent of the world it is as remarkable a global phenomenon as, say, the Internet, that it uses to further its cause. Which is solely that of communication. But in India the word has baggage, it can be an uncomfortable reminder of the past, especially when it is used vaingloriously, as it often is.

Power corrupts and the voice of power has its own false echo. Once I went to a village outside Calcutta to a conference on puppetry. Some was in Bengali, some English; the speakers were all city people, academics mainly, who like to show their solidarity with rural folk with a learned discussion in the heartland. It was in the village hall and to my surprise on the notice-board I saw a large announcement in English among a host of Bengali notices: it was to do with village matters and clearly for people of the community in general. But no more than a handful would have been able to read it. (The language will be spreading its root in the country for several generations yet.) As it happened I found myself talking with the member of the *panchayat* (organ of local government, village council) who had put it up. He agreed that very few would be able to read it. I said it was important information that should be accessible. He seized on 'important': that was why it had to be in English. Impasse.

There is a fairly massive use of English by the more privileged classes to exclude. It is not a conscious procedure and it may well be an inevitable one, given the country's history. A certain class-consciousness is rife in any case; and the infectious nature of the language in basic form may impel the elite to accentuate the polish of their difference. Institutions such as the British Council, that I gave a few readings at in Calcutta, seemed to wrap themselves in a cocoon of pukka English and precious class mannerisms. The ethos of that particular institution is fuelled by a UK funding that appears somewhat gross. No authentic creature can break from this cocoon, only a rarefied class insect that will merely increase the divide between town and country, as between town and town, the have-nots and the haves. Fortunately the changing economy of the world will lead India in time to reject such funding, and such weary imitations of a past power, and find its way, that will include an Indian English way. By which I do not mean an unsophisticated use of the language, though to some extent it will be a new one. But there were exasperated moments when I saw the spread of English not as infectious in the neutral sense as to the end-effect, but as a deadly infection, a plague; and lost perspective and raged.

*H*ow I wish I could plunge my hand in, wrench
a sickening poison-ivy out by the roots!
Rip clear a beautiful leaf that death-pollutes,
its subtle conquering glint – its hidden stench!
If only it could be turned back to its shores,
this army of cells – this gung-ho all-invasive
alien tongue! God is not more persuasive
than this charmed word that kills in countless crores.
Still let the natural flower grow. But proud
in a village hall a notice-board is loud
in letters that few can read, but still a code
for Queen Victoria, Queen Elizabeth ...
while South Calcutta suckles, on Theatre Road,
the British Council's little bit of death.

38

I loved the balcony of the new flat. I would sit out on it at any hour of the day or night, and especially at sunset. Dusk comes the year round between six and seven, in a suddenness of twenty minutes, after a sheet of hearth-fire across the west. The main part of the narrow platform was north-facing, so that one swung one's head left to catch the 'heaven's embroidered cloths' at dusk and right, on the rare times I made it, at dawn. Yeats' lines catch the marvel of the changing overlay to the dull Earth but not the unshielded brightness nearer the Equator. Sometimes I felt, for the colours alone it was worth spending one's days in the tropics.

Round the corner to the east was a shorter platform, and all along it after the slightest of gaps, a tremendous *krishnachura* tree. Among the English-speaking middle class it was sometimes called the 'summer-flame' tree, though the term is now out of use, for the magnificent red flowers it brandishes at the start of the warm months. It was our friend the year round, and in its three months of bloom, an exclamation in laughter. Each year a crow's nest would be laboriously built, a little out of reach of the balcony, often on what seemed the flimsiest of resting-places; but the birds knew how to use a fork in a branch to lodge a precious cargo safely through storms, and a nest never came adrift before its time. We saw the eggs brooded over in the nexus of Nature, the thin beaks cry to be fed, the casual departures. The *krishnachura* shared its open secrets with us and in a sense ours with itself: the *holi* riot of spring with powder flying everywhere, our conversations, our quietness, and all that grew or stayed awake in the silence out there. I imagine that wherever each of us may be, it will stay, a lasting ally, in our minds.

The sky was close. Birds wheeled in and out of the great robe. Crows were everywhere, Calcutta's trademark, but above them kites and vultures often circled, and occasionally a convoy of white storks passed by. The birds of prey tended to stay high but once a vulture alit on a window-ledge a little way opposite and while perched there spread its wings; they seemed to cover half the wall. On the balcony I read and worked and brooded, and seemed to make connections there, whether on the way to a verse of translation or simply mulling over the past. Looking back I think an atom of knowledge found me there, round about my sixtieth year, flimsy as the crows' nest and unshakeable, to settle in, if only for the duration.

Storms were something to watch from inside. But once I stood on the little platform with P. and we saw a localised storm within a large cloud that took up about a third of the vista before us, lightning zagging within the white, while to the side the sky was a calm blue. Rain brought chaos, raging against the stone as tubs of plants went tumbling in the wind. All too often it crept under the door despite the pipe (often blocked in any case). Meanwhile one would watch the street outside disappear and the water level ever so slowly rise. From anything from a few hours after to a few days, the street drain would play its part again.

When we first moved there the newspaper boy would throw up the papers. We took three, two English-medium and a Bengali, and he'd dismount from his bike, swiftly roll up a paper, tie it with a length of string and hurl it up. It was at the limit if his range. Occasionally I'd manage to catch it; more often it fell short; sometimes all three would land in a perfect sequence; sometimes others in the road would have a shot. Unfortunately once one hit one of our windows and broke it, so the less turbulent stair route was taken thenceforth. The boy would cycle through the rain and walk through the flood to deliver the goods. As would the *dudh-wallah* (milkman). The area was a quiet one, but with an eirenic energy, to coin a phrase, beneath the surface. Always, in a Calcuttan *para* (small local area), something untoward can occur, a street disturbance of one kind or another; but at the same time there was a secure sense of community, at least in this corner of Jodhpur Park. I had not felt it in my previous lodgings. It was a good place to be.

At festival time the local committee commandeered all balconies with strings of lights of various hues. The electricity bill was split among the households. More privately, at Diwali we lit candles all along the platform ledge. There was never complete privacy there, though the houses opposite were a little way away; a lot goes on on the flat terrace roofs of all houses, hanging clothes out and the like; and in any case in India one is never alone. But for R. and myself those few square metres, disappearing round the corner to a few more, in the lightest and easiest of ways were treasured ground.

Looking out from there deep in night I gradually found I had another painting in an inner gallery. It is Calcutta at night, the tall office block with one or two lights on, the intimate shapes and spaces, the glimmer of a road, the softness of a park, and the great *krishnachura* tree breathing to the side. The painting must itself breathe the night into any room it hangs in, the dark in its wakeful wholeness, its clarity, its richness, its presence. Perhaps one day I will try and paint these pictures that hang, nearly to the last detail, in my mind. But perhaps they are better left undisturbed.

It was the strangest thing. At some time in this flat, over a few months it seemed, I was in touch with Shakespeare. We met on the streets of London a number of times, he always had some time to talk, then he was on his way. He was voluble, a little swarthy, and gave the impression of being in something of a hurry. I towered over him somewhat. For the period of our acquaintance it was fact, with nothing marvellous or strange about it; when it was over I realised that it had to have been a dream.

It didn't feel like a dream, more as if a parallel universe had come into play. Something similar has happened once or twice before in my life, the experience discarded as real in a literal sense only because it can't have been. We talked as people with an interest in each other's lives, what the other was writing (though no details remain alas), who the other was. It was more than a casual if not a close friendship, and even if altogether absurd from the outside, it is there, a privileged memory in my inner life.

When I came to write of it I found Tagore there as well, Calcutta and London were one, I seemed to have run across them both from time to time. There was a gentleness to Tagore, a hesitant courtesy. A tall man (which he was) he would pause, smile, talk briefly and go soon, always with somewhere to be or something to do. The drama did not extend to whether they knew each other; and the later figure was there only while I was writing the poem. The earlier remains, something that happened rather more definitely.

I was welcomed by either as poet. My output is of course risible, unmentionable in the company of theirs. But maybe after writing poetry for forty or so years with an entire commitment to the beauty of its mystery, I was honoured somehow. I see I have pre-empted the mystery of my own poem now. At any rate it may serve as a reminder of the inexplicable at the base of every situation, in a perspective in which a journey from city to city is nothing, to be who you are is all.

Two friends I have above all friends on Earth.
A small dark man, going here and there, I meet
on London's way. And one of nearer birth,
his mood preoccupied yet angel-sweet,
who passes me with scarcely time to greet
here in Calcutta. Yet it is the same street.
And three, four hundred years can be one day.
They know me, love me, go by on their way.

Who are these strangers met upon the path
of poetry, this night of poetry-famine?
What eye-touch has a hint of a word-heaven?
As if I had a poem or two to say
briefly they meet me, though they cannot stay.
And one is Shakespeare, one Rabindranath.

39

It was before I moved to Jodhpur Park and fell to brooding in my balcony chair, that I realised something about the two miraculous poets at the ocean bed of my being, Shakespeare and Tagore. On the face of it, it is impossible. The voice behind the lines is the same. Of course in Shakespeare's main work, the plays, the personalities are manifold; and Tagore's plays come nowhere near his either in intellectual or dramatic energy, or in poetic excellence. Tagore's plays, as his short stories, are piquant, finely executed, sometimes infinitely moving; they carry his greatness in a minor key. The same may be said for other areas of his artistic expression. It is as a lyric poet that he takes the stage in splendour. But I would not attempt to rate the *oeuvre* of either poet, let alone find them matched in some way. It is in tone not output, a *cri de coeur* of the renunciatory self, a humility merely intensified by the poetic ego that each has in abundance, that they are one.

After I had translated a number of poems from here and there in Tagore's work I decided to engage with his most famous volume, the 'Gitanjali', and succeeded in rendering

all 157 poems into English verse. As mentioned earlier
this is a collection of religious lyrics to most of which their
author added a melody, changed the text to an extent and
so turned to songs. That is how they tend to be known; but
outside West Bengal and Bangladesh, they are famous in
Rabindranath's own English rendering (of a third of them
together with others from other books) in a charged poetic
prose. Still the original Bengali volume has always been
very much treasured and in a loose rhapsodic series the 157
can be taken as a single long poem of a thrilling power. As
I went from link to link on the chain I heard again and
again the unmistakable tenor of Shakespeare's voice in the
Sonnets. I had studied these almost obsessively at college
and over the years they had interwoven themselves in the
backcloth of my mind. With a small handful of exceptions
the series of 154 (whose published sequence the author
was probably not responsible for) have a figure within
them recognisable from one poem to the next. As if in
a new clothing it is there too in the 'Gitanjali'. It knows
all the shades of *dukho-shukh*, as Tagore has it, the heart's
dark and light; it is errant, angry at times (Shakespeare
more so); in touching on Beauty and Time and Death it
is also, in a sense that I cannot put my finger on, in touch
with infinity; it is able to offer itself, with a generosity so
complete as to be almost casual, in the service of love. In
the two collections with all the difference in the world in
foreground and background, intent and style, and beneath
the difference and as if from the root of the common being
of the species, the figure speaks.

An artist gives up the self for the art. No other way can
a work of art come into being. A surface is lost, a surface

returns. Where the human capacity to feel, to think, to experience, to know, to discover, is greatest the submission of the self is greatest too. At the human limit it may even create the same voice. I believe I hear it also in Beethoven's music. But as this is all a matter of the subjective judgement it is time to let it go, something of possible interest noted and clicked from the screen. (Right or wrong in any case it is an observation of next to no intrinsic use.)

For about four years in Jodhpur Park I cycled round on Sunday afternoons to a friend's flat a couple of miles away in the back streets of Jadavpur. We would spend two or three hours at work on a translation of a book of autobiographical essays by Tagore, pass the time, and I would cycle back in the dark. The two journeys were wildly different. Out was a quiet jaunt through suburban streets, back was a nightmarish cacophony of buses and taxis and motorbike-rickshaws with a throng of shadowy pedestrians gliding more or less at the side. In fact once one knew the conventions it was safe enough. I would get back home mildly exhilarated after the careful head-work on the text. Devadatta, my collaborator, was a natural scholar who seemed incapable of mental exhaustion.

He was a confirmed bachelor losing a twenty-year war with his widowed mother, who wanted him married. The capitulation came, a wedding was arranged, took place, in due course a baby was on the way, and suddenly the mother-in-law was at war with the bride. My impression of the mother had been that of a shrewd and pleasant lady; the bride was someone I would have thought incapable of giving offence, with a softness to her personality that should have made living together – as of course they all were – a pleasure. But brides and mothers-in-law in India are a classic recipe for discord; and Devadatta found himself ejected from the flat he had always lived in with a wife eight months pregnant. In a hurry they found another flat in the neighbourhood and a son was born – no doubt what the old lady wanted – and social relations continued between her and her son's family. From the outside it seemed simply a case of my friend's mother being unable to adjust to a situation that she had longed for. Devadatta took it all in his philosophical stride.

He was in fact an engineer who worked as a manager in the city's electricity corporation. He had very little time off – a six-day week is the norm in most jobs and he was sometimes called out for emergency duty on top of that – and yet he gave his one free afternoon to our work of translation. He would not hear of accepting money for it. His father had been a renowned professor and he was cut from the same cloth. I could never understand why, after excelling in his studies, he had not taken the same path, but the world is full of people who at a vital moment have chosen an improbable direction and lived with the result. Once he used the word 'dour' to me with the correct pronunciation. He had never lived abroad, and I asked him how he had known how to say the word – it was not one he was likely to have heard. He told me he had looked up the pronunciation, as he did with all new words, when he had met it. He was quite amazingly thorough, and at the same time sensible to nuances of rhythm and the like in a phrase, in English as in Bengali, and always ready to talk round a point as well as launching directly into it; so that I soon regarded it as the greatest privilege to talk and work with him. The work itself I found special: six essays by Tagore, most of which had been given as talks in the latter period of his life, that centre on the poet's quest.

Tagore is able to look at this head-on, with regard to his own life, without being didactic or dry. He can always accommodate the reader. We took it very gradually and I gained a certain illumination from the journey. When some years before I had finished translating the 'Gitanjali' I had had a transient sense of all my bones, bar the head, bathed in holy water. Now as if at the touch of a faraway hand I felt primed for the business of ageing, as person and poet.

Devadatta loved words. Though I never learned to talk Bengali at all freely I learned a good deal about the language, and especially from him. At that time I had not abandoned my original aim of fluency but I was too lazy to pursue it properly. I did not compromise however in my translation work and every phrase of prose or poetry that I turned to English in twelve years in Calcutta – that came out in due course to several books – I weighed, I believe, with a fine balance. But there were times nevertheless I longed simply to speak the language: it was so close, yet so far.

*W*ill she be mine? She hides: I am on her island:
    darting behind each clumsy piece of air
she is never seen. But I hear a beauty of words
and I sense a lithe tuned body of a poem's song-words
a sweet springing-up, a muscled array of words
in a sparkling of streams I am one with a brilliance of words
in the air I drink in a mother's milk of words
in berry-fruit sip at an ever-new tang of words
the sea around roars with a mystery of words
I will never know. But a beating heart of words
is mine is not mine will it be mine? This beauty
darting before me now yet behind all the trees
of my brain, has her island within me. O let my tongue
sing a new love-song, word-song, speak in Bengali.

40

There were a couple of white women in the Jodhpur Park area (a fair-sized suburb) but I was the only white man. The women were European divorcees or widows of Bengali men and appeared at home in the locale, wearing saris and speaking the language with ease. But (as all newcomers find out) it is a hard path to assimilation. I was nowhere near as fluent as they, and was in any case there for the short term: I had always intended to return to England at some point and R. and P. were looking forward to the adventure. Meanwhile I was not sorry to be colour-isolated, partly for the informative experience; but as time went on, more out of gratitude to the community. There was no colour prejudice.

I am talking of the ordinary people at the shops and the market and the side of the road, not the rich middle-class, of whom there were a significant number in the area and with whom I did not get on. The prejudice in their case was odd. They respected me as a writer but did not seem able to come to terms with the fact that I had married a Bengali woman without a string of letters to her name.

They would not visit the house or invite us to theirs. I grew tired of making overtures. But the ordinary people of the *para* (the immediate local district) treated me as someone like themselves, someone with a family and a certain experience, who was making an effort of a sort with the language and was aware of individuals. That was enough. I was not cheated in the market or the local shops, as I had been in the more touristy areas that I had lived in before. I think having been a teacher for so long helps. Without making one gregarious it can socialise the under layer, so to speak. I was not close to any of these people but not so distant either. The years in Jodhpur Park let a pearl form from the repetitive rounds of the day, no more than the memory of a quiet acknowledgement, the tacit acceptance on the *para's* part of one of a number who happened to live in the road.

Back in England with R. and P. I see my own country is more colour-prejudiced than I thought. Here it is the ordinary people, if not the young. But a sea change may be beginning. I write on the eve of Obama's election to the US Presidency. It is not something I could say if I were writing and thinking entirely in prose, but with the advantage of space included in the account for poetic truth, I can see the doors unlocking in the future, Africa and beyond at last fully welcomed to the Western world. It is the only way forward, and in time the balance in outlook to be gained in this part of the world will prove invaluable.

Round the corner from the flat was Jodhpur Park market. For a year or two, till a reorganisation, it was preceded by a massive rubbish-heap, that birds would perch on, cats nestle in and dogs prowl over, of the most gorgeous colours. One would go on to the half-covered array of shops and stalls usually in late afternoon, after the long slow meridian time when everything's closed down, as if into a great tent with its own tranquillity. It was shabby enough, with uneven paths sometimes a little muddy, and rather cramped; and still there was an ease about it. Later the lights would go on and in the early night it would have a magical air. The fish section was vivid, bloody, glistening. Bengalis love their sea creatures. I've been a guest at a family meal with six different kinds of fish served up; throughout the lady of the house stood at my elbow, anxiously watching my chewing jaws. Is it all right? I could only nod. The fishmongers would sit with their wares in a cheerful barracking-match with their potential customers in which the gleaming heads and bodies under the blade seemed to be a living part. At times the action was silvery-fast yet an exchange never seemed to be merely a commercial one, and nothing was hurried.

We had our favourite market shop. In a tiny area in stifling heat a middle-aged man would stand for hours, deftly extricating all manner of grocery items from piles and boxes and shelves. He had a son at college who with a good grace gave up his studies to help out at the shop: times were hard. Father and son attended to us as to everybody with an integrity of service I envy. I would like to have offered it as a teacher. I would leave a large-ish order at the shop sometimes in the afternoon and one of them would bring it round in the evening with no extra charge. Nothing was too much trouble. After some years the father finally installed a small fan in the shop. Once he and his wife turned up at my stall at the Book

Fair. He insisted on buying a copy of one of my books of translation of the poems of Jibanananda Das. He had no English but loved the poet. It made a contrast with the intellectual family who had preceded him, and whom I knew slightly, who were all over the books with squeals of delight and didn't buy any. My last memory of our friend is his combing his sparse hair before my wife took a photo of him in his shop, shortly before we left. There were shop-tenders and waiters and stall-owners up and down Calcutta that I knew in the more or less limited familiar way one does, and I remember several with a kind of nod of appreciation. But the gentleman standing for ever in the stacked little space where I had to remember to duck my head to get to the counter, is the one we miss.

At the Jodhpur Park flat, as time went by, the family found its feet. R.'s divorce came through, we married, with P. a day-girl at school we were all together. My writing, R.'s project work, P.'s teenage years proceeded with the usual ups and downs. In due course it became clear that the time to make a move to England would be at the end of P.'s schooldays. And so it emerged. But the flurry stays of the flat's first days. I suppose it was a kind of honeymoon (though the marriage came later); at last R. and I had a place that was more than a couple of rooms, and had to sort everything out together from scratch. It was only three months since she had come to live with me in Park Street. Getting the place into some sort of shape had its perils: at one point I found someone from the market to do some work in the living-room and just managed to prevent him smashing into the wall direct with hammer and nail. "You said you had a drill!" "I do, but it's with my brother-in-law." A longer delay occurred in the case of some cowboys who sold me a computer they'd put together, and took literally days to load the programmes. There was some hitch I couldn't understand and nor could they. Finally I kept the machine, that was at a knock-down price, and found someone else to set it up, and it worked well enough and kept going. The landlord got over his manic fit of legalistic pedantry. We forged a partnership with the new place and with one another.

As a child of the country I grew up in Jodhpur Park. Paradoxically the stepping-stone, so to speak, to a firmer footing is in retrospect that childlike moment, a time of grace.

*I*t seems we are flying. Far below
a couple set up house on land:
find tables and chairs, curtains, bread and milk:
and play a kind of serious hide-and-seek:
from time to time, inside their new domain,
they stumble on each other. We see their antics,
these bodily forms; we know,
we who are no more than a winging-at-one,
of a game that's played. For we
are our own gods, exist in our own time,
travel a universe in Creation's light
each instant new. At times we too are seen,
when those two children touch and are at one:
and then forgotten, in our living-together.

41

We were visited one evening by someone who behaved oddly, insisting on leaving just as R. served up a meal she had taken some trouble over. He was a retired professor of about eighty whose abrupt departure meant another, younger friend, his 'wheels' for the evening, also went without his food. They both had English connections, the professor through marriage to an Englishwoman (who had returned for good to her home country) and the other with years of medical practice in England in the past. The professor did not appear to have taken offence, merely to desire to give it, as if on a whim. He was known for such fits and starts of unexpected social behaviour; and eventually knowing him became too difficult to keep up. Yet his eccentricity was a blip on the surface of a mind of the deepest humanity. 'Higher education' institutionalises the mind: its keepers are the world's chattering monkeys: professors the world over operate in a rarefied mental zone that seems gradually to relax its hold on the verities. But Amlan-da was an intellectual such as none I have known, a caring soul who transcended the trappings of university as if they did not exist.

He was an economist who for fifty years had written articles in Bengali and English for the West Bengal press. He had risen to be Pro Vice-Chancellor or Vice-Chancellor of three universities and had published a number of books. His first, 'For Democracy' in 1953, had been sent by the publisher to various international luminaries and was highly commended by both Bertrand Russell and Albert Einstein. The former wrote, 'I find myself in very complete agreement with your ideas, and I think that your arguments against communist dictatorship are such as ought to appeal to those who are hesitating.' Einstein was delightfully measured (I have seen the signed letter). 'I receive many books nearly every day. When I glimpsed at yours I was impressed right away by the independence of your thought and the terse style reminding me of Caesar's 'De Bello Gallico'. I have read the first half of your book with pleasure and agreement and hope to finish it soon. It takes more time than one would expect from its size. If you believe that I could do something to facilitate publication in other countries or to draw attention to it in your own country don't hesitate to let me know.' In his little flat in Salt Lake on the outskirts of Calcutta, that he cleaned himself until a back problem of old age led him to employ outside help, I asked him if he had taken up Einstein's offer. After all, I thought, what young man would not? But he had not replied.

It may be that he did not want to be seduced by the career prospect that could have opened up. He once muttered to me something about Indian scholars who run away to the West. I read a great deal of his English writing, several books and over a hundred articles, the latter as I suggested to him a selection might be of interest to many, and found myself landed with the selector's job! With his permission I tried quite hard to find a UK publisher for the result, a collection of twenty-eight articles from 1953 to 2000. But though a few publishers were interested in the Einstein letter I suggested as a frontispiece, none was in the far-ranging exploration of evolving society that the book amounted to. The newly independent land was its first concern but a world view is there too. The book was called 'In Defence of Freedom' and subtitled 'Exciting Times and Quiet Meditations' and was published in India by the National Gandhi Museum in New Delhi. It is no ordinary economist's work, for the content is entirely accessible to the layman. In an age when the density of scholarship can reach black hole proportions it is a ray of enlightenment.

Gandhi and Tagore appear in it frequently. Often at odds in their public discussion of India's situation and needs they nevertheless were as one in a burning commitment to the country's future. Either one 'closer than half the trunk of a tree' to the other, as I imagined it, these two 'hold all India's greatness in their branches'. Their friendship is a riveting one. Gandhi's vision was the more powerful, Tagore's the more practical. Amlan-da's book, remarkably, does justice to each, though it is about far more than their concerns or personalities. He was a Gandhian who saw early on the shortcomings in outlook of the recently assassinated martyr, and warned of a misuse of the 'mystic temper' that lay at the back of the vision. Just as Gandhi was quirky and peremptory at times so he too became, in a life not dissimilar in the simplicity and depth of its patriotism. He too has fasted more than once in protest at injustice, and the press has taken note. Another economist from the state, a little younger, has been Master of Trinity College, Cambridge, and won the Nobel Prize for his work. Comparisons are odious; yet I dare say the one who stayed behind is as deep a thinker and fine a writer, no less gifted or giving.

'In Defence of Freedom' has much to say on the socialist concept. In a land with a raw and bloody need for development, newly independent, the voice of sanity is to be heard if the forces of extremism are to be kept at bay. Marxism, Hinduism, Islam, property and wealth, tribal society, varieties of humanism (as one chapter is called) – all and far more are deftly traced, in an evolving tapestry of India, against a deeper backcloth of Europe, China, America, Russia. I knew, as I read the many articles, I heard the voice of a true Indian sage. The state of West Bengal permitted its airing, on a narrow enough frequency, the country caught the faintest echo, the wider world not at all. Before things became too difficult with Amlan-da I used to see him every now and then and he was good enough to comment on some of my translations and other verse. He had a marvellous knowledge of poetry and knew its place in the current. As a young man he had known Jibanananda Das (then middle-aged) and had acted as secretary for a literary magazine that Das had founded. He told me how once he had watched Das walk down a street. The poet instinctively avoided people's presence even as he passed them and they him, the very figure of self-effacement. I learnt much from Amlan-da, of inconsequential matters and of the philosophy of humanism, in his words and by his example. A *sadhu* is a holy man who has renounced society and seeks the soul's liberation. Amlan-da was anything but this, and yet at some remove, and despite the offence it seemed he could not help but give, I saw him as such.

The suffix -da indicates an elder male figure to whom one feels close. It is time to give this great man his name. Amlan Datta delivered a talk at the end of the millennium that looked ahead. I went to it, after a year of the planet's media issuing forth a stream of millennial verbiage, and as I listened to the frail figure in the hall, I felt a few such voices are enough. We live in a night of error but with someone, somewhere, to sense a way forward, we have reason for hope.

*W*hat millennial song can be uttered in darkness?
        The old world turns in a day-long medley of bells
spilling the night's note. Caterwauling in blackness
a New Year pealing-for-peace. Hi-jacked by yells
the human word. Is this the next century's carol,
this bungled note – the curse of quarrel on quarrel?
This the pitch of the next ten centuries' music?
The only remedy the mediaeval physic
of conjuring right with might?

                        But I have heard
a singing still, a sadhu's *truth-quiet word*
look at the plain case for an enlightened folk
in a new time. A sky-alert diagnosis;
a visionary heart. So for an hour he spoke
at century's end: and at his elbow, roses.

42

Through a friend of R.'s I came across a remarkable book, and determined to meet the author, A.R.Foning. 'Lepcha, My Vanishing Tribe' was the result of a lifetime's work. As I wrote in an article for 'The Statesman' it is 'a book written without ego, a labour of love. Love in the first place for the truth. The true Lepcha myth, the true history: what can be known and set down.'

As I have said the Lepcha tribe is one of the oldest in India. It has its own language and script, and though it is fast being assimilated by Buddhism and Christianity, its own shamanistic core. Between fifty and a hundred thousand Lepchas remain, in Sikkim, Nepal and Darjeeling District; not all speak the language, whose survival in India is not backed by the government; and it may be a gentle people is soon to be a footnote in the subcontinent's history. I went to Longku village, where everyone is Lepcha, and found that Mr Foning had recently passed away. But I was made welcome by the people (who did not know I wrote articles) and, as it felt, by the mountain they worship, Kanchenjunga, omnipresent and nearby.

A difficult path wound into the village, where hens and chicks seemed to dance at the doors. I learnt that every household has 'a cock and hen, a pig, a goat, a cow'. At once on arrival I found myself drinking *chee*. A fermented drink of millet grain that one takes from a wooden container via a bamboo stalk, it was offered and accepted several times that day. I loved it. But presented with it on waking at 6.30 the next morning I had to decline. If there is a next world, it is my private opinion it is there. Lepchas return to Ney Mayel after death, the paradisal land they come from somewhere on the great mountain, to the arms of Itbu their tutelary goddess. I do not know if *chee* figures in it but I know they would not take offence at the suggestion. Tolerant, practical-minded, humorous, they do not seek to impose their outlook on others. Their society seems to tell of an age before the planet became morally regimented. If and when the tribe vanishes, and may it not be for many generations, one can imagine the good old Earth acknowledging the fact with a sigh.

Over the *chee* offered at my arrival songs of welcome were sung by a young musician and householder who accompanied himself on instruments he had made. He was known as a guru despite his comparative youth (about 30). I was told that status concerned wisdom not age, and accepted the rebuke. To my bewilderment there was a short official ceremony conducted by a *bongthing* or Lepcha priest. I had read of the *bongthing* who mediates in various ways between the human and divine worlds, and of his rarer, usually female counterpart, the *mun*, who can be possessed by the spirit of one who has passed away. Now a pleasant elderly gentleman read with striking authority from sacred Lepcha texts in a rapid lilting tone. Later I was allowed to look at a collection of sacred books. Typically each was a stitched-together bundle of oblong pages bound in coarse deerskin. The fine black lettering had quite faded in parts and other pages were half-eaten by insects. They may have been 200 to 300 years old. My query as to the age was met with various estimates but as I made it I wished I had not. I needed to be there and elsewhere at the same time. To open the treasury, to turn from page to page of the gesticulative script, was better done in silence.

I was taken to the cemetery. It was at the top of the hill the village was on. As I laboured, trying to saunter, a polite escort of young men sauntered, trying to labour. Everyone in the village, old and young, seemed as sure-footed as a goat. The cemetery was a modest enclosure, open to the winds and next to the sky, a most noble spot for one's bones. Nearby was a holy place where Nature is worshipped each spring. The whole village comes up for this. Painted eggshells and small baskets remained from the last occasion. Then a wild thrilling ramble over a number of small hill-tops. I felt the presence of Mount Kanchenjunga other than visually, though it lay before us. The sense was deepened in the evening when a 'cultural programme' took place that everyone came to. Out in the open with a kerosene lamp to take the edge off the darkness the mountain was worshipped, the birth of the Himalayas described, people and Nature celebrated as one, all in dance and song. (Called upon to contribute I inappropriately and unintelligibly sang 'My Bonnie Lies Over the Ocean', a standby of old.) Many things call me back to India but none so much as the touch of belonging to the dark height that I felt in the gusting air and the ground and the circle of faces. I have heard that electricity has lit up Longku now, but as long as there are Lepchas on that patch of land, it will not be a part of the lurid tale of loss, in terms of what we are and where we have come from, that is so much a part of the modern narrative.

No-one got much sleep that night. A series of conch-shell hoots sometime after midnight was interspersed with a loud gabbling at every single door of the village. It was a visit from a witch-doctor of a village some little distance away who made the journey annually to defend the households from evil spirits. The prophylactic words were not wanted in Longku – he was not Lepcha and the superstition was no part of Lepcha belief – but they were endured, and paid for mainly in vegetables collected the next day, for the sake of friendly relations. The community was not offended by the words for it was able to look behind them.

I was sorry not to have met Mr Foning, though I did in a way in his book. He had been educated at one of the St Xavier's Colleges and wrote English as if he had been born to it. It is the merest trifling coincidence but a sentence in his introduction was the same as one in my 'Song Offerings' preface: 'At least this has been my aim.' I was talking of translating Tagore and he of bringing to life on the page a tribal history and culture. But from that moment, all through the book, and in Longku too, I felt a kinship, as if a hand on my shoulder.

There is a certainty of existence, that takes a harmonious, non-aggressive form, that individuals in every culture discover but the culture as a whole rarely promotes. With a lack of intensity stemming from a deep-rooted security the Lepcha way, that has something of the Indian way, has offered an unsung moment in the quest that all of us, from whichever tribe, are on. In an undeliberate journey towards what Gandhi called 'a science of peace' such a clue, and there are others like it, are with us for a time as we rush into economic overdrive. I submit something I was told of the Lepcha culture that I have no reason not to believe, and that chimes with all I know of them. They are not a prudish people and yet the language has no swearwords. There are many places in West Bengal I shall never say goodbye to, and one is the open space in the dark as Longku sang and danced to something older and greater.

*F*riend, I have met and missed you. But your friends
    have met me here with Lepcha love. The hills
remind me of God's gift. No good thing ends
because its case, its nothing-body stills ...
but where it came from, richer there it tends.
Go to Ney Mayel, land that Itbu fills
with innocence. I have met your love, your skills:
I have read your book, and what your book intends.
Your words will keep a story past all change,
a picture that will never lose its look.
Your tribe's simplicity is of the Earth
like Kanchenjunga. Theirs is the finest birth.
You were gone before I met you. But your book
speaks volumes, in a world's dark mountain-range.

43

We cannot look at the natural world. The construct in us changes its nature. We can be of it, and know that being in us; and in our instinctual awareness, it is at once an individual note, and the tap-root of our harmony, to be a part of its flowering. In a sense in India I learnt what I knew but saw it a little more. I offer the recollection of a few moments in part for a dubious anecdotal value and in part for a wry acknowledgement of the random and casual workings of Nature, the flips of its hand.

I used to go to the Victoria Memorial in the city centre sometimes at midday and sit on a bench in its tranquil gardens. Raised a few years after the queen's death the memorial is a building of remarkable grace, a development away from a Western-style city hall in the direction of the Taj Mahal. A stern statue of the old lady greets one on the outside. I was fond of it. One calm afternoon two young men took up the rest of my bench and sat quietly for a time, after which they began a mellow soft crooning, one part against the other and no words, that I listened to enchanted. I was certain it was a religious offering of a kind, perhaps associated with the time of day, and when they fell silent ventured to ask them if the song had a name. They looked slightly embarrassed and finally one answered, " 'I'm So Sexy, You're So Sexy.' "

Then there was the time I went to Pushkar in Rajasthan. This was back on my exploratory trip to the country. I got off the bus and found myself in conversation with a priest who had clearly been waiting for a tourist to usher around. I went along with it. He took me to a very beautiful lake over which I could see the one temple in the world (as described in the guidebook) at which Brahma, the Creator of the Universe, is worshipped. He answered my questions and I counted myself fortunate to be there on a lovely afternoon with a knowledgeable person who spoke my language. So when he asked if he might chant a Sanskrit prayer and that I should repeat a certain phrase at his bidding I agreed. I had no idea if what we said was 'right' but I took it on trust. Then an interesting sequence took place. "Are you married?" "Yes" (as I was then). "Name of wife?" I told him. The repetition came round in due time with my wife's name added with 'happy' (the English word) in front of it; I repeated it as asked. The same happened with the names of my children, one at a time. He broke off to congratulate me on having two sons and no daughters. I said I wished I had a daughter. We continued: and I felt, why not? Forget the Western mind which sees merely water and stone and someone after money. Let the three of them be happy. After a number of repetitions of the happy three so close to me, and the rest of the mantra, suddenly a new phrase crept in, "Happy Donation." At which I stopped, thanked him, and offered the small sum of twenty rupees. He appeared shocked and asked for something like ten thousand. I didn't budge and finally he accepted the twenty. I had begun to be hypnotised and he had miscalculated my defences. I have since met an Indian family who met the same fellow when on holiday there and gave him five thousand.

And there was an epic encounter on a lavatory wall in the Hotel Maria. I had begun to urinate when I saw a huge spider on the wall, and then a gecko lizard stalking it. Not wanting to disturb what was going to happen I was about to suspend operations but let the clatter carry on – act naturally, I thought. The *tik-tiki* made a dart and the spider wrenched free and scuttled off minus three legs. Later that day someone in an adjacent room to mine reported seeing a great five-legged spider. For whatever reason the moment has remained one of the most vivid in the memory.

We can look at the destruction Nature carries out on a greater scale. In 2001 a terrible earthquake killed thousands in the state of Gujarat. I went there a month later and ended up writing an article and a poem. I find I can leave what I have to say about it in what I wrote then.

India has a way to meet the cosmic force all about us and stay 'on-side', so to speak. More as an expression of intent in life, than in expectation of privileged treatment, avenues of recognition are opened up. Men and women admit themselves, in the use of holy name and ritual, into the power of gods and goddesses.

One such is Vishwakarma. He is the divine architect or engineer. The supreme worker, all craftspeople honour him, everyone with their own shaping work, a niche of

whatever standing in industry, all professionals with tools
of their trade. A prayer may be said to him at the first use
in the day of any implement used to earn one's wage: a
factory machine, a photocopier. On his day in September
taxis will be decorated with great vegetable leaves. As
in any celebration there may be impromptu dancing in
the streets. Once on that day I saw a man and a boy of
about eleven lighting up the pavement to radio music.
The man took a break now and then and all eyes were on
the boy who was dancing like nothing on Earth. He was
exhilarated as only a child can be, a whirling dominance,
a spinning brilliant atom. Another imperishable memory,
that seems to celebrate the charge of the city's life at the
side of the road, that boy gleaming dancing.

A patchwork of observations. I do not know how to
express the link between the mind that sees and the world
that is. As individuals we get it wrong, or are of comical
irrelevance; as a society at least we may affirm the bond,
and reach beyond a separated outlook, by time-honoured
word or action. Perhaps there is a further point of vantage
for the individual. I went to a house near Longku that
Tagore liked to visit in his old age, undergoing the arduous
journey from Calcutta for the pleasure of the place and the
company. Maitreyi Devi was his hostess, then a woman
in her twenties, who had been close to the poet since her
mid-teens. He had the gift of discerning another's spark
and had befriended her as she reached out to understand
the world, a gifted young poet herself. She had married
and moved to a hill station with her husband; and Tagore
(whom all her life she regarded as her guru) came out to
her home at Mungpu a few times in his seventies. It was

at this now deserted house that I sat on a tall old battered chair with a rounded back – that I thought might have housed the musings of a more distinguished visitor than myself – and wrote a poem. I was sitting outside, with *jhau* trees behind me and red tiger lilies all around, overlooking a sheer expanse of hills. What can I say? It was as if, for an hour or two, I was in on a secret passed on to the loner, and open to all.

P oet, I think of you when I look at leaves
    dancing before the hills. What hidden event
exultant in its motherhood, brought them out?
Touching each with her finger as if to say
it's time it's time – who on Earth took the trouble?
How do you know her? Then what fathering power
lay in the hills? What long-ago eruption
led to this lightness, childrening all the land?
Poet, how did you meet that potent one
that first-propelled all, and does not age, but still
keeps his whereabouts to himself? Was it here
when you were old, was it here at least once
with that girl scolding you behind your back
you liked so well – you were told of Creation?

44

Maitreyi Devi later became a writer and forward thinker and activist of note. She co-founded Khelaghar, the school for orphans that I had taught at for a time, in a first-floor classroom open to the trees. I did not meet her – she died in 1990 – but heard much about her, and all that I had heard was forgotten as I read a memoir of hers, 'It Does Not Die'. It is an account of an episode in her life at the age of 16 and its painful re-awakening 42 years later. Again I was reminded of the privilege it is to meet someone upon the page. I was taken into the whispering heart of one of the great love stories of the twentieth century.

In 1930, a Romanian student came to stay at her house in Calcutta. He was 23, a gifted scholar in the making and a protégé of her father, a renowned professor who had no objection to the two young ones spending time together. He was ambitious for his daughter as a writer-to-be, and no doubt thought of their acquaintance in terms of a stimulus to her intellectual development and (ironically enough) to her sense of the outside world. Fathers of daughters in the elite households of Calcutta are the blindest people on Earth. The young man in question, Mircea Eliade, became a renowned academic in his turn, and his was the first memoir of the affair to come out, first in Romanian under the title 'Maitreyi' and later (among other languages) in English as 'Bengal Nights'. It is a semi-fictionalised reworking of an emotional entanglement and its conclusion. It came out first in 1933; Maitreyi read it in 1972 and was unspeakably hurt.

It is more than meretricious, there is something vicious in it. The love affair is turned into an egoist's fantasy of himself as a sex god. In 'It Does not Die' (first in Bengali as 'Na Hanyate') Maitreyi replies with a frank and generous factual account that was to tear her apart from the family she grew up in. There is something a touch precious in it throughout; and the ending ducks its own challenge. The book is an extension of the diary form, switching from past to present. She recounts the events of the far past and the near, after she has come across 'Bengal Nights' and suffered a breakdown. Typically she resolves things and arranges to be invited by the University of Chicago to lecture on Tagore. Mircea is now a professor there of the History of Religions.

They meet. He is turned to stone by his sense of guilt and shame. The stage is set for a word of true love from her, a surpassing act of forgiveness. But (on the page at least) she does not find it; but avoids the issue, and makes her way back to her country.

Her book is a very beautiful one, even if ultimately it does not bear out its title. The truth of the affair is clear. In the moment of her awakening all those years back she did not sleep with him, let alone visit his bed night after night, as his lurid imagination set it down, in the novel that based itself on his stay in her home and used her name. There were some kisses, and once she allowed him to uncover her breast and lower his face to it. This admission on her part in 'It Does Not Die' in the 1970s shocked the older members of her family beyond measure. Her younger sister never spoke to her again. (Her husband, it should be said, was wonderfully understanding throughout.) By chance I met the sister in Calcutta in the 'nineties, on another matter, and the old lady talked at length of the disgrace Maitreyi had brought to the family. She sobbed hysterically at the shame of it all. When I left she had recovered her composure and said to me in a normal tone, "I would have liked to have worked with my sister." She was a Sanskrit scholar and I did not know if she meant an intellectual co-operation or work based on social reform. She may not have known either. She has now passed away too. As a little girl of eleven she had played a part in the drama, betraying a kiss that she had witnessed to their parents.

In the crisis that followed Maitreyi told her mother she wanted to marry Mircea as he did her. Mother was sympathetic but Father went into a boiling fury and kicked Mircea out of the house. One of the very few moments that ring true in the young man's novel is what happened next. He walked and walked through the streets of Calcutta and out for about fifteen kilometres till he came to the temple of Kali at Dakshineswar. He had thought the parents would welcome him as son-in-law and the striding stumbling bewildered youth on the crowded streets and hot road could not have been made up. Another stroke of the pen that must have been taken from life is his disgust at the girl's affection for Tagore (who was then about seventy). The boy misinterpreted it of course: in both books he comes over as ungenerous. But Maitreyi's love for him as mirrored in 'It Does Not Die' is undeniable; and not once does she seek to encourage the reader to think ill of him. The third echo of the situation as it surely was, in Mircea's book, also present in Maitreyi's and underrated in both, is the demoniac force at work in the little sister.

Of course she cannot be blamed for it. But what seems to have happened is a deep jealousy of her *didi*, her elder sister, combining with some kind of precocious infatuation for Mircea on her own part, in a psychic reaction that for a time threatened her life, and ended in the infliction of the direst of wounds on her sister's. In the months that Mircea was there she fell into a decline, sometimes passing out, sometimes going into a fit, often requiring Mircea to come and hold her hand. On one such occasion she made Mircea come and kiss her on the forehead and between her shrieks told him to kiss Maitreyi too. It was this kiss, later reported by the little girl, that led to the rupture.

Maitreyi and Mircea both married and led successful lives, as did the sister, who when we met did not refer to her own part in the play of events. From the arrival of the young Romanian at the Calcutta door to Maitreyi's leaving his in Chicago some forty years later, one feels the lives interlocked as in an obtuse triangle, one angle out of sight. All three are gone now and time runs on. A story stays.

I have learnt of pain in Calcutta. Often a woman's hurt has seemed to fill the wandering sphere of my being.

Calcutta, London, nowhere, it is not the place, nor is there a time, it is a part of the human story. The two sexes, the one mind and heart, a closed-in horizon, an endless churned-up battleground. It is not the place, but Calcutta told it to me, at a time when I could hear it, and walking about the city, and sitting on my balcony, at times I felt close to something intangible. It is to do with women's hurt and men's too and children's; and the pure endurance, as if of an individual with her own burden, of a patient part of the Earth.

In my poetry if I speak of a presence, a mother, a lady, it is not that it is not male, but the mind's way is narrow and words are few. In prosaic terms I know there is no tutelary power attached in some way to a city or a country or to myself. But in prosaic terms I know there is no story at all, merely a chance continuation and an inevitable decay. Maitreyi Devi, whom I did not know, is of the dawn for me. There is no divinity, but if there were, it is by a play of Nature, a magical touch of the elements in their round, that I imagine it happening. To pin the idea to a name is to make it ridiculous; but if one thinks of the nameless legions of people the name can represent, it is less so.

*L*ady at dawn, open your eyes to a city
   under a curse. In the delicate hour
you come to the walls. You breathe, and minds are woken;
before each home a curtain is drawn back,
and dullness yields to the quick hands of colour.
Lady at dawn, can you not stir a city
out of its chains? Touch at a dungeon's doors?
Open a pathway to an imprisoned heart?
But go to the dark spots, to the unsanctioned stations,
to a dead law-court, go to Writers Building;
go to the offices of elected power
and look, the long day down, at death. O Lady
still you take into your arms, and kiss with your light
a city under a curse, and free it again.

45

Kali's Temple at Dakshineswar was a good choice for Mircea to turn towards. Together with Belur Math, the headquarters of the Ramakrishna Mission the other side of the Hooghly River, it makes a place of light and serenity for the bruised soul. There is a sense of awakening to it more than of repose. The dual site is at once a place of pilgrimage for Calcuttans (and very many others) and somewhere to go to on a day excursion. Ramakrishna is a Bengali saint of the nineteenth century, priest at the Temple after its construction, and the Mission in his name was founded by his disciple Vivekananda, who is deeply revered and honoured in his turn. The two figures are a part of India's recent spiritual history, and of the essence of Bengal; so that to know of them is not altogether unlike sharing a kinship with the legendary divines of old. They are woven into the present epic, a family of greatness to which an Indian is attached by birth, that joins with the past, a series of living moments that exists like a hinterland to each one's individual journey.

This is regardless of objective truth. Whether Hanuman,

the monkey deity, leapt from the mainland across the sea to Lanka to start the rescue of Sita from Ravana's clutches (I have seen the footprint that he left taking off), or whether Ramakrishna saw God, really is not the point. The account of loyalty and a dashing bravery on the one hand, and an epiphany on the other, in the context of a story that cannot fail to move, and of a life that has enriched millions of people with its insights, has poetic validity. In some respect this is taken on board; and variously by such a treasury of privileged moments in the near past and the far, locality has its own deep anchorage, and nationality its hidden meaning.

Ramakrishna (1836-1886) was more or less illiterate. Unusually for the modern era a mind of genius was left to find all its range in speech, free of the trained focus of the written word. He came up with a number of homely sayings as to the nature of God and man. One of my favourites, that might be a motto for the next UK Budget, is: "As water passes under a bridge but never stagnates, so money passes through the hands of 'The Free' who never hoard it." The German Max Müller, the Frenchman Romain Rolland and the Englishman Christopher Isherwood all wrote about his life, the first also listing the sayings. The most famous of these illustrate his passionate conviction as to God's openness. In many memorable ways he said the same thing: that no one creed was right and another wrong. For an unlettered man to make inroads on the conservative Hinduism of the time with such a radical view was extraordinary. After his death a young man of a different cast of mind, who became known as Swami Vivekananda (the title indicating spiritual mastery), took on the mantle. He was a brilliant scholar, who made a vivid impression at the Parliament of the World's Religions in Chicago in 1893. In a speech beginning "Sisters and Brothers of America", he cut a remarkable figure, an Indian sage inspired by the light of an anti-sectarian torch. One wonders if any of the assembled company were able to take his words to heart. But support for the Mission came his way.

Vivekananda had his own distinctive contribution to make, not so much to theological debate as to the cause of being Indian. He wrote and spoke of a pragmatic, forward-looking approach to living, that welcomes scientific advance, and deals with matters of entrenched prejudice in a straightforward way, still basing everything on Vedic insights of the pure and formless One. He died in 1902 at thirty-nine. In the pantheon of great minds and souls of the city and the country the place he occupies is at one and the same time that of holy man and a figure for the future, much revered and as much admired.

Until writing this chapter my thoughts on Ramakrishna in particular were less generous. He practised a kind of self-hypnosis and declared the degrees of trance-state he arrived at as stages of awareness within a divine spectrum. While he can appear hysterical his disciple can be seen as aloof: it has taken the writing of this account for me to overcome a superficial prejudice against them that I have harboured for some time. It is the vision of Ramakrishna and Vivekananda that is so important. The temple at Belur Math that the latter put up has Buddhist, Islamic and Christian elements. In the space to re-build on Ground Zero, after the 9/11 attacks on the World Trade

Center in New York, could we not have had a mosque, a synagogue and a church? As I write India is reeling from attacks in Mumbai, almost certainly the work of religious fundamentalists. There is an understanding and a tolerance deep within the country's psyche, massed with internal contradiction and atavistic impulse as it is, that will militate against an over-hasty reaction, and lead the region away from danger. In the seething world in one land at least there is a precious drop of humility. It is of value even to recognise it.

There is a quality to a number of the images to be found in the Mahabharata that may have a bearing on this aspect. The author Vyasa has a remarkable eye for comparisons: I sense the truer poet in the similes and not the narrative. He is occasionally given to descriptions of the carnage of war. The battlefield blossoms like a lake lovely with white lily and blue lotus faces of beheaded warriors. Bloodied faces are as lovely as split pomegranates, their teeth like seeds. Warriors target Arjuna like countless bulls attacking a single one to mount a cow in season. Like a monsoon field with red *shakragopa*-beetles, or a young dark-skinned girl's white dress dyed with red turmeric, or a free-roving courtesan flaunting a crimson dress, crimson garland and gold ornaments – such was the earth. (Translations from P.Lal's version.) The artist of beauty is detached from the horror. No statement of any kind has ever spoken more deeply about war than the Mahabharata, one feels; and the freedom to depict the gorgeous colours here, seen too in the noting of the lust to kill Arjuna as a lust to mate, is a thread in a web of contradictions that go to make a resilient whole.

It is what India is. My journey into it, continuing in this account, is beset with cultural bias, a lack of humility on my part, and simple ignorance. The first of these can go the other way. I knew a young chap, a fine scholar, who at the age of twenty seemed destined for the West. A Bengali who had studied in an English-medium school and was now at university, he aspired to authorship in English and had already written several short stories. After two degrees in English Literature in Calcutta he obtained a scholarship to an American university and is now an assistant professor in California. He is writing steadily and beginning to make a name for himself as a novelist. He has not – and could not – give up his attachment to things Indian, his Calcuttan background, his Bengali being. Like my daughter P., a British university student, he is exploring the world. But when he left for America I felt impelled to write a poem asking him to remember his roots. Now after many years there he may be aware of the 'old casuistry' endemic in the economic superiority of the West; or more likely he simply does not see it my way. At all events, as I can discover at times a precarious kinship with Tagore, or Jibanananda Das, as a matter of fancy, I can see him too as a younger brother of mine, going a different way.

Young man of India, across the sky
a horseman of a newer age rides by.
He carries on him deeds of property
bequeathed to him by ancient family,
and goes to claim a newer territory.
His is the wealth of the next century,
for him the West unlocks its treasury,
a gleaming coin of mental wizardry.
He travels near to that rich destiny,
that glittering stardom of prosperity,
that owes too much to an old casuistry.
Only recall your own land's poetry,
I ask him as he rides on, far and high,
young man of India, across the sky.

46

In her full glory the ten-armed goddess Durga carries ten weapons. These may be a sword, a trident, a thunderdisc, an arrow, a javelin, a club, a bow, a noose, a goad, an axe. To confound the buffalo-demon who threatens the universe she stands in the *pandal*, at the instant of crisis, in shining array. At her feet the sinuous demon coils, buffalo-persona to hand. He is always quite a fellow, good-looking, and clearly possessed of a devilish strength. While her younger son Kartik, god of military tactics and youth, stands to her far left in distinctly less masculine attitude, something of a fop in fact: the comparison invariably is an amusing one. Though as I write the words I know it may not be to the Bengali. But my faith in Durga reaches beyond the difference of cultural background. She is there on our behalf, in a festival-moment now to last out this writer's act of homage. For the remaining chapters of the account let her stand till as image and brief witness we come to an end.

While I was there India became nuclear. In May 1998 she conducted a series of tests at Pokhran, near the

Pakistan border, and declared herself a "nuclear weapons state". What would Pakistan do? The opportunity to take the moral high ground, in the eyes of the rest of the world, was massive. If she had not followed through with her own programme to develop the nuclear warhead she could have milked the West for favoured status (and the USA for a blank cheque) for as long as she liked: but the issue was never in doubt. Just as India, in her own eyes, had at last become a nation to be reckoned with, so too the viewpoint of the rest of the world meant nothing to Pakistan. Within three weeks she had followed suit.

All I knew in Calcutta were glad that India had taken the step. There were two or three gentle souls in particular I had expected to question its wisdom: but all were in accordance. There were in fact a number of protest meetings and dissenting voices; yet among my acquaintance none, and that seemed to be the general mood. India had come of age; and who was Britain or America or France to lecture her on the folly of an action they too had taken and not renounced? It had to be: and President Clinton, who appeared bewildered by the event, might have reflected on the hard facts that will always lie beneath the notion of a sisterhood of nations. It is something the new President-elect of the U.S.A. will have to consider when dealing with Iran. The power to destroy may be held up but it will surely come. All that matters is the power to act responsibly.

Durga has a part to play in the balancing-act of the time. She understands war; she understands peace. This is to say, her country subsists in a state of feverish health, a zone of travail that finds a way forward, whereby something of her very great experience may, in the course of things, become available for other countries to draw on. A drop of restraint.

The frisson of violence is never very far away. Two or three of my middle-aged acquaintances, sober respectable bodies, turned out to have been Naxalites in the 'seventies. This was more than a little student unrest. In Naxalbari, a small village in West Bengal, a Communist Party splinter group formed from an uprising against the local landlords, and quickly organised itself with a Maoist animus. The underground movement took fire in the metropolis. 'Class enemies' were assassination targets. Guns were rife. The Marxist wing of the Party regained control and was elected to power in the state, remaining so for more than thirty years to date. Still in Calcutta passions seethe, eyes light up, voices drop to a whisper, as greybeard memories re-ignite. The fever is there and the knowledge of its quelling. Wisdom needs madness.

As I have said before there is a politician in the state who has tried to counter the grip of the CPI(M), the Communist Party of India (Marxist), and it is for no display of wisdom or of madness that I bring her up now, nor of the two mixed, but merely for an anecdote with an indirect bearing. I went to the Esplanade once to hear Mamata Banerjee speak, a place where great roads meet at the hub of the city. There were about a hundred thousand people there. She emerged onto her platform to the megaphoned strains of a song of Tagore's, *ekla chalo re*. "Go on alone", says the title, "out alone, out alone, out alone, go on alone". Sung slowly as it was, it is a haunting echo of the fight at the heart of things human to discover one's individuality. Yet it was not (after the first incredulous moment) out of place. My initial reaction, yet again, was the outsider's, rather too ready to see a certain humour in the situation; then it was oddly moving. India knows of the lonely plains of the self, of what goes on if nobody is there. The incident is an example of the 'double take' the visitor is never free of; and may reflect on the theme of fertile contradiction, the quickening paradox. At any rate it is yet another moment to remember the roads of Calcutta for.

Another anecdote: I am in the Delhi Durbar, a restaurant off Sudder Street, Calcutta's tourist hot spot. Two cousins run it, Muslims, loud, big-hearted men in their thirties; it is always enjoyable to eat one's breakfast there. One morning however it was not. There was a furious argument going on between the two of them. I couldn't understand a word – it was not Bengali – and ate on, edging my legs aside as the cleaner wiped the floor under the tables. The argument rose in pitch. As the cleaner emerged on his knees from a table he got an almighty slap round the face from one of the cousins. He carried on with his work. As he came into view later the other did the same. Slowly he carried on cleaning. I could swear the argument had nothing to do with him; there had been no gesture in his direction or apparent reference. They wanted to hit each other so hit him. The cleaner had shown no sign of understanding the argument himself; but there was no mistaking his own role. The next morning the cousins had recovered their customary bonhomie. The cleaner did his work impassively.

And a more sobering instance of male brutality. Three women officials of the West Bengal Government (Health

Department) were travelling by car, on duty, in the outskirts of Calcutta (Bantala) when they were surrounded by a mob of men. Their clothes were torn away and they were attacked. One died in hospital; the other two survived after remaining in a critical condition for a long time. Their driver died trying to save them. There was no apparent reason – some said there had been a rumour of kidnapping in the area and people were wary of strangers. Though there was no mention of rape the attacks were of a sexual type and they were bitten all over. When asked to comment the then Chief Minister for West Bengal said, "These things happen a lot," and the then Health Minister said that women should not travel so late (8pm). In a way the ministerial response of educated men was the worse atrocity.

One cannot duck the issue. A male viciousness savages the planet. I believe that Durga, and India behind her, may stand for a new impulse in the struggle, a new kind of seeing. After Pokhran for a moment it seemed a version of the old story had taken effect, power for power's sake; but I cannot help but think that as likely is an as yet unwritten chapter on the international scene, where knowledge is used as it should be, to inform a richness of action, to be and to let be, to create.

*S*omewhere the air is on fire from her pure fury.
Somewhere the new-fangled killing weapons are released
from her lovely hands. In immaculate deployment
spinning-discs and studded clubs and new-tipped spears
(chemical and biological insanities, nuclear hells)
on a sacred seeking-out, will clog the air-space
and still the humble field. India if you are worth a name
do not imitate the brazen goddesses of other lands
for a name, that smallest thing, has the ring of love
in its use, in its thought, and in its very letters
the thread of friendship gleams on a billion wrists.
Somewhere another shining is at hand
O goddess of Spring, goddess of flowers, who seek beyond
with eyes of a new truth, weapons that are not blind.

47

The flat terraced roof of an Indian house is a boon at night. In Jodhpur Park I sat out under the sky for hours at a time. The lightest touch of space can free one from the invasiveness of things below, the fixity and drag of the norm, that clings to one like a uniform. Sometimes with R. and sometimes on my own I would savour the coolness, the lilt of the moon's presence, the shapes of trees and clouds and buildings, the thrill of a city at rest. It is a place for a kind of elastic thinking: one can let oneself go for a moment, to revel in the namelessness of all things, and return to an enriched view, a sense of dormant epic, the story we continue and create. The wide concrete rectangle with the low parapet wall one could perch on became a necessary escape, and soon a place of sanctuary. But we had to fight for the right to be there at all.

When we first saw the apartment we liked it and quickly came to an agreement with the landlord. The roof was up a further flight of stairs and as an afterthought I said I looked forward to being able to go up to it. The landlord (who did not live there) said it was out of bounds. He was withholding the key. "Why?" "Children from the road will run up and play there." It was a quiet area though of course there were children about, hardly a threat it seemed; and in any case I promised to lock the door faithfully when it was not in use. No deal. So I called his bluff, said we would look elsewhere, and he came round. It was still some months after the move before he gave us the key, one of a number of power plays that disappeared when he finally saw we were responsible and let his guard down. As far as I know no children ever came into the house unauthorised at all, far less set out to rampage on the roof. To a Westerner it may appear he was concerned for the children's safety. One can't say it was nowhere in his thoughts; but the sudden no-holds-barred wrestling-match we found ourselves engaged in the moment we had taken the flat spoke of a behavioural switch I had met before. It might be called the flat hand of the Calcuttan landlord.

On the roof, then; and though they were not visible from it, I would like to recall a few spots on the Calcuttan scene as if I were up there one last time and could see them. I am cycling to a little restaurant, Sutripti, to meet a friend, Nimai, who had a meal with Jibanananda Das there in the early 'fifties. It is on Rashbehari Avenue in South Calcutta, where the poet was fatally struck by a tram a year or two later. We always meet there in India. Nimai was a student then; now more than fifty years later he has an encyclopaedic knowledge of the arts and artistic figures, of the West as of Bengal. Yet following the death of Jaya his wife what I have learnt from him of the matter of the soul, merely from the snippets of his memories, and the shaken state he has undergone, has eclipsed by far the sporadic commentary, invaluable in itself, he has offered on matters of the mind. All the gleaned knowledge in the world on artistic works, and the figures and movements behind them, is as nothing beside an incalculable depth of experience of love and suffering, that I have seen a glimpse of across a restaurant table. The table has been in London, where he also lives and where we have often met, more than in Sutripti; but it is in the little place where he talked with Jibanananda, that our conversation started and to my mind where it carries on. I unlock the bike and wheel off as he walks heavily away.

I am waiting at a desk in Writers Building. Its owner is waiting for me outside in the blinding heat of noon. This is the headquarters of the Government of West Bengal and I am to meet the new Chief Minister, a man of deep literary interests, and to present a couple of books to him. But the official who has arranged the meeting and is due to take me to him, a neighbour of mine, is waiting outside. I was due to meet him at one of the doors but was ordered in by security personnel who are everywhere and sent up to his desk. By the time I get there he is downstairs and outside. I am not allowed to go and find him, or of course the Chief Minister. I stop various people and explain the situation. I am told more than once it will be seen to. It isn't. I miss my appointment and my neighbour waits for an hour and almost gets heatstroke. No-one has a mobile 'phone though they are starting to be seen a lot in the city. It is a state of eighty million that is being governed like this. Another meeting is arranged and I see the CM and present the books but almost nothing is said except by my voluble neighbour, so happy the meeting has finally taken place that he stays on and talks the whole time. I think the CM thinks it was my fault the first meeting went astray. At any rate I thank him for again making the time to see me, he smiles, and my foray into the political high life is over. No-one on either occasion has searched my briefcase, or indeed myself. The CM is a gentle soul but I do not expect to hear from him regarding my translations, and do not, more's the pity. Still, I am glad to have been able to present them to him.

In the Indian Museum an old man is singing. I am there to assist in the making of a film about Durga Puja, 'In Search of Durga'. Professor K.K.Ganguly, a venerated authority, makes the past and the present as one with his rendering of a Sanskrit hymn in praise of the Mother Goddess. The Museum fronts onto Chowringhee, the smart main road at the city centre, and backs onto Free School Street, where pigs are rooting in rubbish. Its rooms have a wealth of information and I have often been there, but never learnt as much as from one man's song.

I am arguing furiously in New Market. This is a little covered city of shops next to the main tourist area and anyone of fair skin is fair game. In the past I have paid quintuple what I should have on one or two items. Now that I have 'wised up' and can rattle away (somewhat) in Bengali I tend to do better but it's still hardball every time I go. Yet I love the place. Some years before I came here much of it was lost in a massive fire. It was rebuilt with no concession to modernity and has a dense sense of history and the trading spirit that goes back to the beginnings of Calcutta. Craftsmanship of all sorts, a famous cake shop, ornate chess sets, innumerable saris, kitchen implements, all the stuff of life is here at a price. I cannot glance out over the city without visiting it again.

I am with R. on the Hooghly. A stretch of the holy river, running on past as all roofs rise and fall, this is the water from which the city grew. We pay a hundred rupees (a little over a pound) to be taken out for an hour in the evening in a kind of great punt. Once we saw the corpse of a man drifting down. The river is where my thoughts lie I have no words for. After one has been in Calcutta for a time it includes one or one includes it, and in the most unthreatening and gradual way imaginable, there is the sense of a deepening acquaintance.

Half-asleep once in a chair on the roof I had a half-dream. Kali danced her dance of terrible triumph and Shiva saved her from going too far by lying down before her, but they were young lovers, and Calcutta their universe. What it may be about I can no more than half-say; but the freshness of it, as I opened my eyes, is still with me.

*H*ere on the roof time stops. In the silence
    of a full moon, eyes closed, I can see
the dark one, Kali, somewhere by me.
A city's destiny in the balance
she holds: and slowly now she dances.
A Calcuttan damsel sighs in the air
her wonder love. Then doubt, despair,
a broken heart ... an army advances
crazy and measured in a girl's feet,
then suddenly kicking against the sky
to break the beyond. See a youth lie
beneath the blind passion, to still the mad beat.
What did I dream on the terrace? It seems
a great city's poem moves in my dreams.

48

In Park Street one often heard the *azan*, the Muslim call to prayer, soar out on the air like a warmth in the blood. Muslim communities all over the city follow the vivid pattern of response the call preludes, and living near such an enclave, I too was able to feel at times ritually attentive. A momentary lift, without an iota of the responsibility of the believer; but it sent an invitation, as it were, at least to remember the thousands of good people making their way in the same district as oneself. There were times I caught a hint of a sweetness of life in a Muslim area, both in the metropolis and in the occasional village I found myself in, that intrigues me. From an outsider's position I wonder if it may be allied to a system of internal constraint, widely imposed and deeply accepted. The other side of a coin that is invested in a print-out agenda for the inner life. This is to take a cynical view; as I write I am aware of a residual attraction within myself for the acceptance of an overriding direction. From far off one has a glimpse of a submissive calm. There is a level at which the atheist is always at odds with the believer. While I would not wish to follow suit, I know that the laying aside of the existential burden can be a joy.

It is all religions I am talking about. But – again as seen from the outside – Islam surely needs to take a step to re-define itself in the light of the time. A Vatican II could turn out to be a milestone in the planet's history. Islam in India is tolerant and adaptive in its living practice, but still it can be frightening to the outsider in the militancy of its pure belief. Once in a village outside Delhi, the car I was in was brought to a halt by hundreds of men and boys beating their chests. It was part of a Moharram procession, I was told, and no hostility was intended. Certainly none was directed at the car which was allowed to pass slowly through. But the sight of several hundred males of all ages, from boys barely old enough to walk to aged men, beating their chests to express their grief for the death of Imam Hussein, the grandson of the Prophet, over thirteen hundred years ago, was a touch unnerving. On another occasion I followed a Moharram procession in West Bengal that halted every now and then for youths to drag themselves over glass and carry on dancing down the road, their backs a mass of blood. Others had their faces pierced with pointed sticks, in one cheek and out of the other. All carried on dancing. Girls and women watched from the side. We came to a field where a holiday atmosphere prevailed, refreshments were on sale, people sat on the grass, all seemed at ease. The same announcement was made several times from a loudspeaker. I assumed it was to do with crowd organisation and perhaps the need to move on. It turned out to be a request to people not to kill themselves for grief at Imam Hussein's martyrdom at the battle of Karbala in 680. I was told that every year there are two or three suicides in the area on his account. Some might not use the term 'militant' for such displays of devotion but the states of ecstasy, self-flagellation, even self-immolation associated with such times, are expressive of a militant love, that most Muslims would allow as a core element of their faith. There is no need to play with the concept of militancy, how one aspect may or may not be linked to another, since the underlying issue is no kind of fervour, but rather to do with the repetitiveness of a dogma that feels itself under attack. In some distant time, when we understand more of what words are doing, and more of how the prosaic and the poetic worlds inform each other, all religion may be able to accept both difference and change as part of its nature, and the breed of *homo sapiens* be aptly named.

In the great tradition of Indian seers a Muslim poet in the early twentieth century saw past the verbal fencework that partitions off the godhead. Nazrul Islam was born in Bengal in 1899, the same year as Jibanananda Das, and as unlike him in personality as it is possible to imagine. Nazrul was fiery, exhibitionistic, a showman, but like him, a remarkable poet. No modernist, however; he took the traditional forms, finding no need to deliver a jolt to the system by way of an idiosyncratic style. His poems are marvellously deft, with a Tagorean ease and prosodic virtuosity; as Tagore, too, he composed thousands of songs. He was outspoken against the mistreatment of women, famously addressing a prostitute as 'Mother' in a poem. He wrote of earthly and divine love, of many gods, and of his homeland. A great patriot and revolutionary, imprisoned by the British, he entered a plea to the judge in his case that began, 'I have been accused of sedition. That as why I am now confined in the prison. On the one side is the crown, on the other the flames of the comet.' Some critics call him a jingoist, finding his nationalistic attitude a touch manufactured, his rhythms unsubtle; but more see a gaiety and a freshness in his verse, and a compelling vein of philosophy. He contracted a brain disease in his forties and lived on thirty years more, passing away in the newly created country of Bangladesh, whose national poet he is. He was a Muslim who crossed the divide, one of the great Bengali poets. With three others he made my journey into the language an unsurpassable gift.

They were Tagore, Jibanananda Das, and Lalon Fakir. Lalon was neither Muslim nor Hindu but both and more. Perhaps the greatest of the Bauls, he lived (apparently) from about 1774 to 1890. As a youth he was found abandoned and suffering from smallpox and a Muslim family took him in. He never revealed his origin, and became the leader of an ashram devoted to a view of Creation and the Creator that dismisses 'the triumphant blast of pedigree-family-religion-caste' as one of his songs has it. About a hundred remain of these, tricky to translate though I have had a shot at a quarter of them, with village dialect words and a kind of rough-and-ready sweetness that has simply escaped me. He had hundreds of thousands of followers: it would seem the Muslim-Hindu divide ceased to exist in his presence. At the last Book Fair I attended, in 2006, I wrote a poem in his honour (going every day of the eleven or twelve) in which he accompanied me through the crowds, at the stalls, we two alone, and told me of his life and sang new songs.

'Lalon Fakir at the Kolkata Book Fair' was the last long poem I wrote in India, a final wave of a cascade. 'Old Baul / you led me here. Your hand is on my shoulder / the rest of my days,' I say near the end, and finally, the gates of the Fair behind me, my companion long gone, 'Old Lalon / shall I catch up with you on an open path / between two villages?'

The sense of intimate acquaintance with poets I take with me from India is something I cherish. If I start to think what else, there is a blurred impression of a good deal, and tentatively, as if of a full moon rising, the shape of a wholeness. I seem to know that it will stay as long as I do and it may get clearer. Of course the mind's need to be schematic and the personality's desire for fulfilment can cook this sort of thing up, and I have no way of telling if it is a mere illusion. It is there and I shall leave it at that.

*T*he sweetest sound is in the air,
   the azan, lifting up in prayer
a dust-dry, city-blemished heart.
Upon the roads I play my part,
a scribbler of no faith. I enter
an unseen mosque, a hidden centre
of soul's release, a certain finding
of day beyond the day's dull blinding.

The call is done. When I have gone
to spend time with my brother, Lalon;
and freed at last from British rule
I go to visit my cousin, Nazrul;
then one poor heart will know the One –
O when the golden call is done.

49

Early in my life the Christian story left an impression on me, like a slight dent, and while that filled out, the memory stays. What reason briskly dismisses as pure folly lingers in the aftermath. The mind cannot dismiss a love affair. It may bring it to an end, and yet it has not gone. In India I had passed the age of discretion, at least as compared to the innocence of childhood, and the love stories of the gods and goddesses there do not encroach on whatever it is my head takes as fact, the bump of prosaic truth. It is an area that is not allowed anything like a privileged development of its own, in the world at large. All too often it is commandeered by a foreign element, to the point of downright confusion. It can take a while for this to clear up. But different areas of the understanding use different processes. The abacus of the daily reckoning and the rosary are not the same instrument. It is also true that Hinduism is a less dogmatic religion than some, less absolute, more in accord with the imaginative freedoms. I was fortunate to meet it when I did and fortunate to meet it at all.

The deity most associated with West Bengal is Durga and a sense of the Mother fills the state as it can few places in the world. The drama is of epic proportion and of ordinary human experience at the same time. In the line-up of the goddess and her children on the great screen in the *pandal*, in Ganesh's marriage, Durga's fight with Mahisasura the buffalo-demon, the family visit and the family departure, the living status of the characters of the last four great days, and in the constellation of ritual moments before, after and during, a reality is acted out. It is theatre, and the stage is the road and the home, the foreground of everyone's life. At the root of it all is I believe the struggle of a woman for every one of us, the protection and the delivery, the heroic animal labour. At an unspoken level lies a recognition of something the everyday world must forever take for granted.

Be that as it may the festival of Durga Puja resonates from first to last with a note we hear all too loudly the rest of the year: the chime of darkness, the massing force, the threat of reversal. At the same time the pulse-beat of anticipation of the arrival, and the tenor of love, of benevolence, of triumph, and finally of sadness at the departure, sound together and rise above it in a superb hymn. The first time I witnessed the festival I wrote a long poem, 'Meditation on the Goddess'; the second time I took part in a film, 'In Search of Durga', that in good Calcuttan tradition was never screened (a little was sold to a Swedish television company). Thereafter I went *pandal*-hopping, as they say, always interested in the arrangements of the images on the *chalchitra* or screen; and otherwise took little active interest. But writing the poem and especially making the film, that presents a Calcutta far removed from the needy and distressed place in so many Westerners' minds, took me to the heart of a old tradition. Each year I knew the goddess was there, I was sad at her going, I knew she would come again. For the rest of my life if ever I go back at that time, I know beyond a doubt I shall be found by her there.

I have spoken of an intimation of Parvati in the hills, her light step unseen. While from outside it may seem curious to be on any kind of terms with a divinity if one is atheist, and with a lady of fluid identity at that, in India nothing could seem more natural. As Durga she is dear, as Parvati delightful, as Kali deeply necessary. It is Kali who tells me I must go back to India. Her garland of skulls calls me. As a people we make gods, and they can inform the person. If we allow them to they can unite us with Nature, or with one another. They can remind us of the very current of being, that is also of non-being. The River Ganga is a god too, and may have been one since people have been able to speak and bless the Earth. Divinities are our creation, and to know of them, as of some kind of living presence, is to take part in the role-play of the species. There is no need for the atheistic outlook that is gradually evolving to preclude this. The stem-cell of the human imagination, that has allowed the thinking animal its organic regeneration for so long, is excised only with fatal consequence. But it can be seen more clearly for what it is.

A god who stays in the background in Durga's visit is Shiva. His face looks out from high on the *chalchitra* but unobtrusively; a mere sign of his presence, as he waits in

Kailash in the Himalayas for his wife's return. He is of course Kali's husband too and Parvati's; I have said nothing of him except as husband; but he is infinitely more. I find I do not dare to speak familiarly of him. Brahma is the Creator, Vishnu the Preserver and Shiva the Destroyer. Within a family one or two sometimes will follow Shiva and one or two Vishnu, with not a hint of rancour: a personality choice. Brahma is not followed in that way at all. I have unfinished business with Shiva. Everybody has. He destroys to make way for new creation; he is the god of dance, of time too; the male force in pure form his body is at times a pillar of fire, extinguished only by the vessel of the mother-goddess; he is at once the householder and the detached yogi, absorbed in meditation; his throat is blue with swallowing poison that would have destroyed every last thing on Earth. From far, from very far, I follow him.

It is time to take a step back. It is India, the crowd of a billion and more, I have come to know a fraction. The gods and the poems, imprints of the imagination, are not the place and the people, the population in front of one. While I was there it crossed the ten-figure mark. I was not at ease, by and large, living amongst it. I did not get on wonderfully well with several of those I knew. The reasons are various, some applying to my life in England too, and not unconnected with the simmering need to write. Though I did not speak of it much I constantly felt in a slightly skewed position, a dilettante Westerner and a Britisher at that. Even in my lifetime my place of birth had been the governing power. I had the sense of a botched transmission, as if India could not fight free of the past, to take hold of its new being. But for all this, I came to feel accepted, at a deep level, into the country. I felt I had come to know a little of India's greatness, and of the immediate and passionate strength of the people all about. Despite my shortcomings a way had opened for me, across a border, into a second land.

O ne billion souls. To have entered this household
is to have taken the warmth of a holy flame
on my face and hands. India I am washed free
of a shadowed being.

What is this endless seething,
scrabbling, snarling in a second-hand cage?
Where is the good arm to knock down, re-build?
Where is the clear eye to inform the mass?
What is the blindness in the family pattern?

Has it not been my fault, the poet's way
to trespass with truth? To hover inside a doorway
half-seen, saying too much, silent too soon?

A threshold is behind me. Mother your flame
billioning-in-one, bids me towards its breath.
I bow to its inevitable power.

50

In retrospect a moment when I touched base in India was in the translation of the sonnet-sequence of Jibanananda Das, 'Bengal the Beautiful'. Its mysterious sense of the present and the past together, with an interlacing of myth and the natural world and village life, seems to speak from the very heart of the country. Hints of a personal story give it an all too individual poignancy. It might be any one of us saying it. It is a moment I take with me of restless peace, a tangible reminder, merely, of life in the mind, a breath of existence, unsettled, settled, a tremor in a current.

Such is poetry. Das is a modernist with a style that takes full charge of its material. When this does not happen, as in the work of many an experimentalist, the style can be irksome, forever babbling to the reader of a special personality behind the words. When it succeeds it is the time that is made special. Jibanananda's sonnets look outwards as well as in. The individualism is in a context, the new time with the old, Nature's richness and a sharp particularity of place. In among a host of presences, figures of myth and history, the village and the thicket, is the dreaming eye of an alert soul.

It is a love-poem, a man's delight in the ground of his being. To read it is to be filled by the passionate murmur of an Indian silence. Another poem that celebrates the land is one of Rabindranath Tagore's offerings in 'Gitanjali'. I wish it had been used for the national anthem instead of a song Tagore wrote on another occasion, that is full of noble sentiment but lacks the swing and pulse of the 'Gitanjali' piece. The latter goes to the heart of the nation. It shaping force is there, its openness, its pride. It has an uninspiring melody that I do not think was Tagore's: I like to imagine it sung with the *brio* it deserves. 'O my soul, awaken slowly / in this holy pilgrims'-place, / where India's greatness reigns, before / the ocean's space,' it begins. The starts of the succeeding verses indicate the range. 'No-one knows from where it flows / or who set it in motion, / this wild flood-force of humanity's course, / to mingle in mid-ocean.' 'All in uproar, awash with war, / and singing victory's song, / past desert-track, over mountain's back, / they made their way along.' 'Of old upon the heart-strings rolled / *Om* in its great sound / unending where the One in prayer / rose ringing all around.' 'In the holy fire-maze see now ablaze / sorrow's blood-red flame. / As it burns in the heart, to bear it is our part – / it is written beside our name.' 'O come Aryans, come non-Aryans, / Hindus, Muslims, all, / come all of you, you English too, / come you of the Christian call.' Tagore wrote it in 1910, before the movement for Independence took fire but after he had become politically involved against the English with Lord Curzon's vivisection of Bengal into West and East in 1905, reversed in 1911. In full the poem (I have quoted a little over a quarter) seems magically to find the Indian thread, through far and near past, to a future of a certain human richness. Each verse ends with two lines from the beginning (that took a number of attempts to translate): 'where India's greatness reigns, before / the ocean's space.' Throughout a voice seems to speak out of a diversity of peoples, to name a common experience, with the unspoken sense of a fierce endurance, and the hint of a renunciatory love. It is a patriotic poem like no other.

Tagore knew of the One. A holistic vision comes to us from his works and days that would appear to allow for a certain development in the way we conduct ourselves as a world society. It stems from his practice as a poet and the hand of genius he displays in a variety of artistic forms. His insight into the needs of society at state, national and international level, and his energy in the realms of the imaginative, led to an unusually active personality. I think he illustrates the way we all can be, and indeed the way we all are, in a more or less unrealised fashion. The mind and the world rest on a duality of action, a continual inter-nourishment of two truths, the poetic and the prosaic. Tagore's ability to take an empirical approach to what needed doing, that he applied to considerable effect to what he saw about him, drew on his commitment as an artist (in the widest sense). There is feedback in the reverse direction; but it may be that it is from a base of artistic practice of some kind, that the motive force for change is at its most capable, and the good things get done. One day we may look back to Rabindranath as the precursor of a way of being at once more original and more active at large.

He used religious terminology: the One is the divine. As things are I find I can use it in poetic mode. By which I mean allowing the imaginative world to impose its reality, as at festival, as well as when writing a poem. It is time to abandon the discussion of what we do with words, or of a hidden means of the mind in preparing the ground for action, and to count one's blessings. What other word is there for it? First, there is a certain train journey I used to make out to two stops on the same line, from the first year of my stay to the last, that throughout was like opening a door to an area of special significance. The journey was often tough, and my friends in the two places – two teachers I first thought of as my brothers – did not stay as close as I had hoped. But it was always a privilege to see them and their families and to walk in the villages where they lived.

Badkulla is a village near the town of Krishnanagar and some three hours' train-ride from Calcutta. Its name means 'No Tax', from a revolt against demanding landlords in the early nineteenth century. Part of my enjoyment in walking in it naturally came from that alone. I was re-acquainted with a simple truth of my childhood there, observing the pace at which life was lived, the neighbourliness, the lack of ostentation. Of course there was a whiff of malice and unpleasant politics about, of neglect by the state government, of all the dark shenanigans of life everywhere; but for me there was something holy there too. My friend Pranesh, an award-winning poet, has lived in Badkulla all his life, and to a very small extent I was able to see it through his eyes, as we walked round. He lived with his widowed sister and her two sons and their house and garden was a place of light. On the way back to

Calcutta I would visit the larger village or small town of
Chakdaha, often with Pranesh, and we would see Alok,
his wife Chandralekha and their two daughters, and
often I would explore the green and somehow mysterious
expanse of small roads and paths on the outskirts where
their house was. They rebuilt much of the house while I
used to visit and allowed me to name it, 'Rup-Katha', or
'make-believe'. On their own 'rup' is 'beauty' and 'katha' is
'word', my cunning tribute to wife and husband. (Alok is
a committed but occasional writer with words at his core.)
I would catch the train on to Calcutta (Pranesh going
the other way), and get home always with the sense of a
fulfilled day, if a little tired.

To be in India was my blessing. And to have my own
family there, to be a father to P. And with the sense of it
at times sweeping me like a flame, to be a husband to R.

O ne soul. One lucid tint behind all colours,
   one pair of eyes on the sky, one flowering tree,
one whispering mind on the way, one gorgeous palace
always at hand, one travelling place to be;
one land to love, one far green wash of light,
one river crashing through Time, one conch-note blending
known and unknown, and one bent head of night
telling, in turn, its tale that has no ending.
Garden of India, one soul dropped by
to write words with the jewel of poetry
upon a glass; to sense, beneath the sky,
what may be God. One world is gifted me,
and something more, to let me know it whole:
the dancing eye-song of one other soul.

51

The goddess stands in a blaze of light. The lion that has brought her is at her side or feet, the demon she is to vanquish is below. Her weapons glitter; her face shines out more; always she is serene, calm, in a word, good. There may be eleven hundred *pandals* in Calcutta alone and each has a different Durga if we look at the outward design. This can include the facial expression, that sometimes is stylised almost to a perfect stillness, and sometimes is charged with a certain seriousness, and sometimes is glad yet never informally so. She never lets her guard down. But while we take in the outward form we are drawn to the inner quality, the same wherever we see her. The tableau of her imminent struggle and of her children on either side, gods and goddesses with their own special attributes, reminds us of the circumstance – our circumstance – and her figure is a focus for that quality we treasure most. In her beauty, knowledge and kindliness it is revealed to us as a pure element, that as we look we do not need to name. But if I had to find a phrase for it, it would be the responsibility of love.

On her far right is Ganesh. He is vastly popular throughout India and has his own ten-day festival in several areas, the state of Maharashtra and its capital Mumbai honouring him especially. He has an elephant head and a benign, almost avuncular expression. Usually a little plump, he has done well and he wants you to do likewise, he seems to say: he supports new enterprises, and may remove obstacles to their success. He is sharp, a little mischievous, capable, warm; there is a man like him in everybody's family. Durga's elder son, he is by some way the most accessible of the line-up in terms of personality; and his being married off to a banana-tree on the seventh day is somehow profoundly satisfying. At his feet is a rat that has carried him on his journey. I have never asked or tried to find out why that is: it is one of those questions one does not want an answer to. If one is in India for any length of time, he is there as a friend.

Between him and the goddess-mother is Lakshmi. She has come on an owl, who is somewhere about her feet, and she carries a pot or urn that may be seen either as cornucopia or as a symbol of thrift. She is the goddess of prosperity and appreciates a well-run household. A good girl is often called *lakshmi meye* or a boy *lakshmi chele*. She is worshipped on a full-moon night in autumn when her owl brings her down to touch the home with fortune. During her mother's *puja* she is a quiet and dutiful young woman in the background; yet vital to the proceedings, instinct with her power, able to bless. Or so I feel as I pause to look at her.

The other side of the mother the lovely figure of Saraswati is poised. The elder daughter, she seems always to the fore, impulsive, finely restrained, as if something in her is dancing or singing. Her name literally is 'the one who flows' and indeed there is a river Saraswati, hymned of old. Her swan is by her; she holds a *veena*, a stringed instrument; she is free and keeps perfect time; to the eye not moving, she is far from still. Goddess of learning, of music and poetry and song, she is not a friend to me, but closer than that: she has news for me I am free to heed or not. She is by me while I am; she is by me while I am not. Bengal loves her; the simplest of people, who value education the most, pray to her on her day. I do not pray to her, but while I have words, I thank Saraswati.

If ever there was an odd one out it is Kartik, next to Saraswati at the end of the line. Yet he is as much part of the family as anyone. God of military tactics and youth, for some reason he is presented at his mother's festival as a dandy. I can never quite see him on the battlefield, nor indeed advising his mother on how to deal with the demonic Mahisasura. He is a bachelor and rides a peacock. If I think of him as a son of Shiva, however, at once I have a certain respect. And to be sure he is his own person, as individual as any. In any case he is there, the great screen unimaginable without him. All are there. The *pandal* pulses.

It is the evening of the tenth day, *mahadasami*. Crowds roar along the streets. The demon has been dealt with, a moment recognised by the ritual sacrifice of a small goat, or more usually now, by the mock one of a fruit or vegetable. The *chalchitra* has been taken out of the *pandal* and circled by married women who bid Durga a farewell as she leaves her first home, as they all have done. The visit to her origins is over. Hundreds of lorries trundle along, bearing dismantled images to the sacred river. Many are packed with excited children too, and have toured the city before heading for the final act, the Immersion. Processions on foot and in slow cars accompany the gods and goddesses on the last stage of the visible journey. Car windows open and "Jai, jai!" is heard on the night air, "Victory, victory!" The streets burn with light, thunder with an intermittent drumming. Something is given up, there is no holding on. At the river Durga is raised and turned three times, a leave-taking ritual, and with her family, the demon too, launched into the water. Boys and young men help to push out the images onto the dark water, swimming a few strokes, turning to shore. The goddess is on her way to her mountain home.

***

I have been filled with images too. Like the *pandals*, now taken down, I have been visited by a presence, to be privileged past belief. And like the images themselves, a thing of clay and bamboo and straw, animated for a time, one day I shall start a journeying-back. If the body is a *pandal*, the mystery of the birth of awareness in it, that is the advent of the personal, is honoured in Durga's days.

India my festival, not of ten days but twelve years, Calcutta my city, my dried-up Western soul has found a story. Now and then it will use it, with thanks; meanwhile I take a phrase with me from a Baul song. *Moner manush*, the Person of the Heart, is with me on my way. Early in India I had the sense of starting over, infancy, childhood, a becoming, a tentative adulthood; all that is over now, or the sense of it is. That phrase, a very few words, that I would not wish to say often (though if I could I would sing it), will stay alive and keep everything alive for me that is in these pages, and a great deal more.

I take my leave of city and country, the Immersion evening sounding in my ears, the silent slow rush of the river before me. I am given to the current. It is the Hooghly, it is Calcutta, it is more than these and further. It is India and more I have been in for a time. All is One for an instant as I go out, far out, to leave behind me a song of the Earth.

*S*he has come to the city, the first one, the Mother,
 on lion-back the loved one, unafraid against evil.
She has come, God-in-Woman, whose eyes tell our power,
whose arm-strength, uncoiled, takes aim in our blindness.
She is here with her children, the dear ones of talent,
to call on us. Lady, we are new in your presence,
with you we return to the house we were born in,
awake in the innocent flowering Earth.

I have come to the river, I am out on a journey,
swept back to a sky-space, stream-swept to a silence
of stars. For an instant I heard the Earth's music,
a drum-beat, a singing. For an instant of star-space
I am one with all singing. A Goddess is near me.

The festival's over, the drum-beat has ended.

52

The reason to go was clearer than the one to stay. I had always intended to be back in England at some point, after living abroad for a time. R. was keen on the move. The date emerged as P. was awarded a place at an English university. R. and I had married and had been to England together a few times, twice with P. R. made sure DANA, the NGO she had set up from scratch, was able to continue (she has been back to look after a fieldwork project, another *chetana-chala* or Awareness Journey). I cannot speak for R. and P., but for me, as I neared my mid-sixties, it seemed the right time to return.

The decision to stay, back in '94, had been merely a hunch, based on the value poetry had so clearly in the living mind of the city, and on something I have no words for, except to call it a summons by Saraswati. (Though when I abandoned plans to travel more widely I scarcely knew Saraswati from Eve.) I regard the writing of this account as a final part of the journey, my own *chetana-chala*, and of course it does not stop there. Whether or not in the geographical place I shall venture into the subcontinent, even if merely by admitting old memories, and letting them steal a march. But I have another journey in mind now, and that is to learn something of the physical world, before it is too late. From a position of common-or-garden ignorance I want to find out a little more of what is going on. Even if I do not write another poem (unlikely) I think Saraswati would approve.

There is much of my time in India I have said little of. The extended family; the travelling outside West Bengal; the journalism; the teaching. Of these the last was in all essential respects no different from my time in schools in England. If the mind of a child is a magnet one turns it towards profitable material that one brings into range. Or one has a great time with young people, following a slightly zany modus operandi in my case, always with the intent of fostering a love of literature and language and accurate thought and usage, and day by day carried forward on a surge of knowing and being known. As with teaching, so with a good deal of what one is involved with in another land. There is a point at which one stops seeing the differences. For the rest of my life I shall take fresh stock of some of the ordinary practices around me. I offer a final few glimpses of India, to pick up the pattern of the day-to-day, and as an adieu; and tell an anecdote of home, that could be anywhere. But first a comment on the presentational mode of the foregoing, that the reader must have found unfamiliar.

It was an experiment, to balance prose and poetry, the one resting on the other, as if riding a wave. The fifty sonnets, that were written in the order they appear here, I called *Guest and Host*, and from more than one point of view it seemed a usable sequence. It is not for me to look at the use I have made of it; in any case, as with much else, it was a matter of instinct. But I hope the juxtaposition of styles, if unfamiliar, has not been a cause of discomfort: that the double strand can find a single weave.

I am in a small holy town at the southern tip of India. The train deposits me at Rameswaram station at about 4am and in utter darkness, following the slope and then by sound and smell, I make my way to the sea. I sit and wait for the dawn. When it comes I see about fifty people standing in the water praying to the sun. I had thought I was alone.

We are putting candles out for Diwali along the parapets of the balcony and the roof.

A superstitious cycle-rickshaw-*wallah* suddenly stops pedalling in the middle of nowhere. A cat has crossed the path in front of us.

In a packed and shaking bus on Central Avenue the conductor brilliantly juggles tributaries of small change onto his moneybag lid in the crowd's midst, without dropping a coin or missing a beat.

I am on a small boat on the Jalangi River in the heart of the countryside. The sky and the water make an open bowl of the afternoon.

R. mutters to a fly that is annoying her in our Jodhpur Park flat, "Go back to your village!" Later she feels a twinge of remorse.

On the train to Santiniketan a fruit vendor with a tray on his head shouts, "Lebu lebu lebu lemon! Lebu lebu lebu lemon!"

I am sitting at my table in the Jodhpur Park sitting-room. It is a room of some size and I have found a table to match: about three-and-a-half feet wide and seven feet long. It is black mahogany, serviceable and firm, and costs under two rupees a day to rent (about twopence). It comes from a furniture shop near Park Street that has a wonderful attic of such items. The owner has in the past made us bookshelves, some chairs, a small table. When we leave for England I beg him to sell me the old black giant but he has had many years of steady income out of it and clearly it will go on for ever. I would have taken the legs off and packed them separately in a crate we had made to take our belongings, into which the top would have slid. It has been a work-companion to my days. I hadn't thought of it before but it may well have been a relic from a house of the Raj. In which case I'm as well off without it.

And another table story. I have hired a smaller one from the same shop, which for years is called 'the putting-things-on table'. This is because R. queried the need for it. "What's it for?" "It's for putting things on." She found this remarkably amusing and the name stuck. It stands by the giant, unused except for spare piles of books I am too lazy to put back on the shelves. Meanwhile P. works without a table in her room. She is in the sixth form now and has essays to write, files to keep organised, and insists on sitting on her bed and writing against a small flat stool on the bed in front of her. I offer her the spare table; a perfect space can be made for it in her room by the wall. Absolutely not. She doesn't need it. I suggest to R. that P. should have it. Absolutely not. She doesn't need it. (I may say that the work-bed culture is not uncommon.) I can't stand it. Finally, when P. is out one afternoon, I simply take it into her room. R. is furious but I carry the table past her, position it neatly, put a lamp and flowers on it, go back to the giant, grit my teeth and wait. P. returns. I hover by her door as she opens it. She turns and gives me the blackest look I think I've had from anyone. I ask her to leave it there for two days and then I'll take it out if that's what she wants. Nothing is said to me the rest of the day by either but late in the evening I hear giggles coming from her room. I don't dare knock but begin to wonder. The next day the mood is lightened but still nothing is said on the matter. Finally on the second day P. admits it's an acceptable change, even a very acceptable one. The giggles were from R. and P. reorganising things in the room and the latter realising she liked the addition. A sweet victory.

We came over in August 2006. The three of us have had much to do. The wave of change never stops. I am making up for all my sitting around, whether on the balcony, at the old black table, or in the garden of the Fairlawn Hotel, by teaching full-time, after more than a decade at two days or less a week. I have been fortunate in the school I have found. R. and P. have their own stories. It remains to offer thanks to a city. One may touch the feet of an elder person as a sign of respect: this is *pranam*. Its hubbub fills me as I offer my *pranam* to Calcutta.